HAFÉZ

HAFÉZ

Teachings
of the
Philosopher
of
Love

HALEH POURAFZAL AND ROGER MONTGOMERY
Abdol-Hossein Pourafzal, Literary Consultant

Inner Traditions
Rochester, Vermont

Inner Traditions
One Park Street
Rochester, Vermont 05767
www.InnerTraditions.com

Library of Congress Cataloging-in-Publication Data
Pourafzal, Haleh, 1956–2002
  Haféz : teachings of the philosopher of love / Haleh Pourafzal and Roger Montgomery.— Paperback ed.
    p. cm.
Originally published: The spiritual wisdom of Haféz. Rochester, Vt. : Inner Traditions, 1998.
Includes bibliographical references and index.
  ISBN 0-89281-188-9 (pbk.)
  1. Hafiz, 14th cent.—Criticism and interpretation. I. Montgomery, Roger, 1944- II. Title.
  PK6465.Z933 2004
  891'.5511—dc22

                                        2003026438

Printed and bound in the United States at Lake Book Manufacturing, Inc.

10 9 8 7 6 5 4 3 2 1

Text design and layout by Kristin Camp
This book was typeset in Bembo with Florens as the display typeface

This new paperback edition of *Haféz: Teachings of the Philosopher of Love* is dedicated, with deepest love and gratitude, to my wife and coauthor, Haleh Pourafzal.

Haleh crossed over into the Realm of Spirit in November 2002, rejoining her revered teacher and guardian Haféz. Foremost among many treasures bequeathed to family and friends was her shining example of devotion to the beloved, a central tenet of her ancient Persian mysticism. The pages ahead, and especially her first-person chapter "One Soul Standing Guard," reveal the depth of her commitment to the spirit of truth and unity that she always found in Haféz.

As we on this side of that mysterious veil continue our own journeys through life, may we all discover that precious nectar of silence and awareness that graced Haleh's every day and helped create this book.

—ROGER MONTGOMERY

Contents

Complete Ghazals

Acknowledgments

Gratitude to Haleh's father and mother, Abdol-Hossein and Nahid Pourafzal, her brother Houman and her large extended family for their unconditional love and support of Haleh's beautiful life and her work on this book. Her passion for her beloved Haféz was conceived within and nurtured by these extraordinary people.

During our work on the original manuscript, Haleh and I received valuable assistance from Mr. and Mrs. Rofougaran in Paris and from David Iino and May Murakami in Berkeley. The first edition benefited from Inner Traditions editors Jon Graham, Rowan Jacobsen, and Blake Maher; it has been a pleasure to work with Managing Editor Jeanie Levitan on this paperback edition.

A special word of gratitude must go to Ron Roth—the man Haleh always called "Teacher"; to Haleh's and my fellow monks in the Spirit of Peace Monastic Community; and to all the Celebrating Life spiritual family. Through Ron Roth's acknowledgment of Haleh as a modern day Persian Mystic, and by the community's appreciation of her teachings through and about Haféz, both the ancient poet and the extraordinary woman live on in so many hearts.

—RM, November 2003

Notes on the Text

Various spellings of the poet's name have appeared in the many translations of his work over the centuries. The authors consider *Haféz* to be the spelling that most accurately suggests the original pronunciation. Other spellings appear in the text when sources are quoted.

The distinction between the terms *Iran* and *Persia* is somewhat vague in contemporary English usage. Iran was the ancient name of a geographical area that includes the current country of Iran, which was so named in 1925. The Persians were one ancient Iranian tribal group, who gave their name to both the nation and culture that emerged two thousand five hundred years ago. In this text, *Persian* is used to describe elements of that culture, many of which exist to this day, and also Iranian persons who trace their family lineages to this unique heritage.

On my grave don't sit without wine and musician,
so that I might wake up from the dead dance.
Hold me tight tonight, spirit, although I am old,
so at dawn I wake up young from this trance.

Introduction

By Roger Montgomery

*Y*ou are about to meet one of humanity's greatest friends and most delightful companions, a man named Shams-ud-Din Mohammad. He lived long ago in the fourteenth century in the Persian city of Shiraz in what is now southern Iran. Shams-ud-Din Mohammad was a seeker of wisdom who became a poet of genius, a lover of truth who has transcended the ages. His timeless message of liberation invites us to meet him in the tavern of the human spirit, to share a cup of wine, and to enjoy a blissful vision of humanity's highest potential. He emphasizes the "enjoy" part.

Shams-ud-Din Mohammad took the pen name "Haféz" and cleverly inscribed that signature into the final verses of nearly all his hundreds of surviving poems. Through the centuries, Haféz has been read, memorized, recited, quoted, and loved by millions of people in one of the world's most spiritually oriented societies. He remains Iran's most popular poet to this day.

Haféz the poet was a synthesizer of knowledge, a thinker about the human condition, and a reporter on his own journeys into higher awareness. Like his Persian predecessors Jalal-ud-Din Rumi and Omar Khayyam, he was a poet of God. But his vision was so all-embracing that his writing serves more as a tool for pointing to the totality of the Creator than as a litany of praise. A superbly educated man in absolute command of the subtle beauty of one of the world's most expressive languages, Haféz traced his roots of reference back to ancient Persia and extended his vision unimpeded into our own future. His mastery of poetic form empowered an endearingly informal style that has preserved his visionary content through the ages.

Haféz wrote of both the wine of the spirit and the wine of the grape. He burned with our hearts' longing and bubbled with our minds' humor. His full-length poems endure as in-depth essays on life, while virtually every individual couplet stands as a masterly homily of simple but profound advice:

> *Let neither pride nor rich delicacies delude you;*
> *this world's episodes extend not to eternity.*

He also blends deep yearning with a thoroughly modern sales pitch:

> *Make this deal—buy from me this shattered heart.*
> *Its worth is more than a thousand unbroken.*

And sometimes he is just wry and witty:

> *Either don't bring home elephant riders*
> *or build a house with a very strong floor.*

Such is Haféz—heart open, intellect detached and soaring, tongue in cheek, a lover of humanity. An incomparable weaver of the mystic and the hedonistic.

On a spring evening at a sidewalk café in Berkeley, California, I sat with two of Haféz's very best friends, my coauthor Haleh Pourafzal and her father, Abdol-Hossein Pourafzal, whose life's passion is the study of the poet's works. Students from the University of California laughed and talked and dined around us. We three shared fine red wine as though the café were a Persian tavern. Our talk could be of only one topic: the master poet Haféz.

"I have been a Haféz lover for fifty years now," Hossein said with a smile. "How long have you known him?"

"Only about five years," I laughed, as though discussing a neighbor down the street. "Haleh introduced us."

Hossein's presence is that of a dignified Persian elder. He is a self-possessed man who misses none of the student activity around us. An attorney for forty years in Iran and France, he now splits his time between Los Angeles and Paris. His favorite spots in the world are the intellectually stimulating environments of coffee houses filled with chattering students. In Paris, where he lives "fifteen minutes by Metro from thirteen million books in the Bibliothèque Nationale," he frequents the Latin Quarter with fellow members of the Persian-Parisian literary establishment.

"There is absolutely no subject of importance to humanity as we enter the twenty-first century that Haféz does not address in his poetry," Hossein said. A lifelong student of Persian linguistics, Hossein is the fifth-generation direct descendant of Ghaem Magham Farahani, creator of the contemporary Farsi prose form. Although his conversational English is fluid, it does not measure up to his masterly and intricate command of Farsi. Since his comments on Haféz must reflect subtle and sophisticated levels of thought, he switches to Farsi, and Haleh translates. "The center of all Haféz's teaching is justice, and humanity is thirsty for justice now as never before. It is the perfect time for his teachings to emerge in the West."

Hossein embodies the same admiration for Haféz that I first observed in Haleh, an admiration based on respect for an artistry and intelligence that serves truth above all other values. This is not surprising, since it was Hossein's daily recitations of Haféz that first awakened his young daughter's awareness of the poet during her childhood in Tehran. I thought back to my own first encounter with Haféz. Our Berkeley office was quiet that winter afternoon. Haleh was focused on a book, and I was drifting into a nap in my favorite chair when she said, "I want to read to you."

I nodded, but my eyes did not open. She sat beside me, paused, and then invoked a flow of words and feelings like nothing I'd heard before. Her voice, naturally rich and deep, entered a rhythmic world midway between chanting and singing. There was cadence; there was rhyme. Her reading drowned all thinking:

Ma bedin dar na peye heshmat o jah amadeim
az bad-e hadesseh inja be panah amadeim.

The language was the Farsi of Haleh's homeland and its great Persian poets. A language not of my tongue, but certainly of my nervous system.

"What does that mean in English?" I asked.

"No yearning for fame and fortune has tempted us to this gateway," she said slowly. "Rather, we come as refugees, guided by cosmic occurrence." Our translation work had begun. When we began to translate in rhyme and rhythm for this book, the verse became:

Neither fame nor fortune tempted us to this gate;
we approach as refugees, here guided by fate.

She continued to read. Tears resounded through her voice. Centuries melted away. Around and beyond the words, drums pounded and flutes strained into outer limits of hearing, while dervishes in white whirled just outside the edges of inner vision.

Nagahan pardeh barandakhtei yaani cheh
mast az khaneh boroun takhtei yaani cheh
(What do you mean suddenly the veil has lifted?
That suddenly you are walking away gifted?)

She read on and on, a priestess calling up magical truths and strangely penetrating questions in harmonic melodies. Rhymed words and syllables repeated continually. Poem followed poem. Rhythms varied; the intensity and otherworldliness of the incantations did not. She finished. I sat entranced, unwilling to speak or open my eyes. After a while, she said simply, "That was Haféz. He is my favorite poet."

Intoxication described perfectly my reaction to Haleh's reading, and I would come to understand that no word could be more fitting. But I also would learn that *sobriety* was equally appropriate—and absolutely necessary—in describing the world and work of Haféz. "I don't have to understand Farsi to know there's a lot more than just pretty words in Haféz," I said as my eyes finally opened. "Can you tell me more about him?"

"You're right," Haleh laughed. "Haféz is not just a poet. He's a wizard, a musician, a singer, a dancer. The poetry of his day was written for performance. If you really want to know Haféz, you must learn to dance like a writhing serpent in your mind. But there's something more. He is a thinking poet like no other Persian before or since. He brings you philosophy, and he challenges you to think on his own level. Many people love his poetry just for poetry's sake, but many others seek the deeper meaning. It seems to me that his philosophy is understood best by people who are free spirits."

From that introduction, Haleh patiently began explaining the essence of this Persian poet and philosopher who had been her most precious source of inspiration since childhood. In Iran, where more books have been written about Haféz than about any other person, it is said that literally every Persian feels a private bond with the poet. In the words of publisher Mohammad Batmanglij in the foreword to the book *Hafez: Dance of Life,* "In Persia, poetry is a part of everyone's life, from the sweeper in the bazaar to the university don. Hafez, one of the great poets, is also the most popular."[1]

Haleh's deep fascination with Haféz spurred me into a personal quest to comprehend more of this thinker of Persia's past. As I scanned various English-language translations and writings, the tantalizing comments of several literary figures caught my eye. Typical were these words from Forugh Farrokhzad, Iran's best-known modern female literary figure: "Oh, I wish I could compose poetry like Haféz, and like him possess the sensitivity to establish a relationship with all the intimate moments in the lives of all future humankind."[2]

The praise also came from nineteenth-century Europe. Deeply inspired by an early German translation, Goethe wrote, "In his poetry, Hafiz has inscribed undeniable truth indelibly. Hafiz has no peer."[3] Among a number of verses Goethe addressed to his kindred spirit of Persia is this:

> *Holy Hafiz you in all*
> *Baths and taverns I'll recall.*
> *When the loved one lifts her veil,*
> *Ambergris her locks exhale.*
> *More: the poet's love song must*
> *Melt the houris, move their lust.*

"Hafiz fears nothing," observed Ralph Waldo Emerson. "He sees too far; he sees throughout; such is the only man I wish to see or be."[4] Emerson composed a few of his own renditions, working from earlier German translations, capturing the Persian certainly as well as any other English interpreter:

> *O just fakir, with brow austere,*
> *Forbid me not the vine;*
> *On the first day, poor Hafiz' clay*
> *Was kneaded up with wine.*

> *Up: Hafiz, grace from high God's face*
> *Beams on thee pure;*
> *Shy thou not hell, and trust thou well*
> *Heaven is secure.*

British scholar Gertrude Bell, who translated Haféz's poetry from Farsi, wrote, "It is as if his mental eye, endowed with wonderful acuteness of vision, had penetrated into those provinces of thought which we of a later age were destined to inhabit."[5]

The praise flowed on. Spiritual teacher Inayat Khan wrote: "Hafiz stands unique in his expression, in his depth of thought, in the excellence of his symbolic expression of certain thoughts and philosophy....[6] Hafiz teaches one to see the ultimate truth and the ultimate justice in one and the same thing, and it is God; that justice is not in related things, perfect justice is in totality."[7] Sufi teacher and author Meher Baba wrote, "There is no equal to Hafiz in poetry. He was a Perfect Master."[8]

Tributes also came from the German philosopher Nietzsche and from Rudyard Kipling, who had access in India to old manuscripts of the *Divan* (literally, "collection"). This book of Haféz's poetry was assembled after his death and today is regarded in the Middle East both as great literature and as a divination tool similar to China's *I Ching*. An obvious pattern emerged in these comments: Many who had access to his poetry in Farsi as well as a few great literary minds who read translations considered Haféz among the finest of all poets.

Meanwhile, Haleh persuaded me to think of Haféz not only as a poet but also as a sage and philosopher *(filsouf)* in the realm of Plato and Lao-tzu and Confucius. From this starting point, both the form and content of this book began to emerge. To expand and enhance our perspective, we welcomed Haleh's father to Berkeley.

"Without any question, Haféz was a genius," Hossein observed as we ordered dinner. "When you examine the entire body of his work, there are six specific indicators of this genius. First, there is his depth of intellect. That is self-evident. Second, he is futuristic. He understands how the future will come into being. Third, he balances every philosophical idea in an appropriate perspective. He sees the need for balance in all of life.

"Fourth, his mind is fluid in the cutting-edge fields of his time. It is obvious that he is educated in algebra, geometry, philosophy, history, mythology, astronomy, logic, theology, literature, music, and linguistics. Fifth, he displays great political acumen. He is deeply concerned with social dynamics and issues of equality and human rights as they existed in his time.

"Sixth, he is a personal counselor. His words offer direct life guidance, and people have continued coming to him for centuries by consulting the *Divan* as a means of divination. Put all of this together and you see a fearless, thinking being of self-reliance, deep resourcefulness, dignity, and integrity. You see a genius."

In addition, Hossein explained, Haféz's brilliance is demonstrated by his use of poetry to break through the repressive religious environment of his times in order to express a complete philosophy of the sacredness of the individual within the framework of universal mysticism. That he chose the rhythmic poetry of the sonnetlike *ghazal* form for most of his composition was a key to this achievement. "In Persian literature, the ghazal was the best pedagogical tool available, the best way to bring ideas to a society. The ghazal was a superior form of poetry—the most mystical, most beautiful, and also the most educational. It was a dancing, joy-creating form of poetry. Messages came across when delivered by the ghazal."

Hossein's eyes moisten as he speaks of Haféz, but he deals in facts as well as feelings. In Iran, he reported, the latest count is about six hundred books written about Haféz. Perhaps half have been published in the past fifty years, and most of them concern the *Divan*'s divination system. Hossein maintains his own mental outline of the sources and process through which this huge body of work came into being. In addition, at the Bibliothèque Nationale in Paris and in other French public and private libraries, there are hundreds of books on Haféz in many of the at least twenty-five languages into which the poet's work has been translated.

UNESCO, the United Nations educational and cultural arm, officially declared 1988 the "Year of Haféz" and conducted a conference in Paris to honor the poet and explore the significance of his teachings for the modern world. This event was initiated by the government of Iran, where thoughtful observers, in the tradition of earlier centuries, are turning increasingly to Haféz for political insight and counsel. As a troubled world poised precariously on the brink of the twenty-first century, prominent scholars from many lands confirmed that Haféz's poetry and philosophy speak directly to our contemporary cutting edges of philosophy, psychology, awareness studies, educational systems, and business theory. It is easy to imagine the old poet smiling at his growing prestige and musing, ironically, that he has been here all the time.

As Haleh and I began to work on this book, Hossein assisted us in many ways, such as gaining access, in Paris and Iran, to an extensive body of previously untranslated writings of Iranian scholars. Many of these scholars have made it their lives' work to study, catalogue, and analyze the entire body of Haféz's poetry, breaking down all the ghazals, couplet by couplet, in order to create an overview of his message to humanity. Hossein provided us with what he considered to be the fifty best Farsi books on Haféz, each offering unique insights into particular aspects of the poet.

One focus of this book is the application of the inspired wisdom of Haféz to the dominant personal and public issues of our own time, this unique period that has come to be known as the Information Age. As the speed and complexity of our daily existence increase at a sometimes astounding rate, we are faced with a continuing need to upgrade our spiritual lives in order to balance the demands made on us by our technology. We have found the wit and genius of Haféz to be an ideal source of inner renewal no matter what draining issues arise during contemporary days. In addition, we have found that translating this Persian verse into easily comprehended modern English provides an effective vehicle for applying the poet's essence and intent to the life of the present.

Most of the complete ghazals translated here come from the Farsi edition of the *Divan* assembled and edited by Ghani and Ghazvini in 1941 and considered by many Farsi scholars to be the most authoritative version. Individual couplets, however, have been selected from a dozen different Farsi *Divans,* each with its own variation of content and commentary. The total number of authentic Haféz poems is a topic of much debate in Iran. Some scholars have attributed more than seven hundred to him, but the most credible sources have set the figure at about five hundred.

The earliest known version of the *Divan*, dated 1391—only a year or so after Haféz's death—is reported to be preserved in a private collection in Gurkohpur, India. It includes four hundred and thirty-five ghazals, twenty-six *rubaiyat* (the four-line stanzas for which Khayyam is known), and eighteen other poems.

Our translations, with rhyme schemes and rhythm patterns approximating the original structures as nearly as possible, are designed to be read aloud, the same as the original Persian versions. The English wording is aimed at illuminating each passage's meaning as intended by Haféz in the context of the full scope of his writings. Our emphasis is on projecting the deepest essence of the poet's message, and often we have chosen to enhance word-for-word translation with English language content that clarifies meaning in a style consistent with the poet's mode of expression. To some degree, our prose is an extension of the translation process, since its purpose is to create an environment allowing the spirit of Haféz to find expression, just as it did in fourteenth-century Persia, with reference points in the past, present, and future.

We have created titles for the complete ghazal translations even though the original Persian poems had none, because we find these titles helpful in creating context for the verses' content. Also, since every edition of the *Divan* differs as to poems included as well as organization and wording, there really is no other definitive way to refer to particular poems.

For Haleh, this book encapsulates the focus that inspired her life. Born in Iran and tuned to the spirit of Haféz, she chose a career in international service management in order to pursue her life-as-service, a key element in the poet's philosophy. This perspective also connects traditional spiritual and philosophical wisdom from the ancient cradle of civilization to a modern vision of the world. It remains our hope, as co-authors, that this writing can serve as a single step in aligning two cultures in desperate need of mutual understanding. As Haféz said:

Peace in two worlds is the merging of two paths:
fairness with friends, fellowship with enemies.

To our two cultures and to each of us personally, Haféz proclaims this message of unity through his every verse. Welcome, the poet says to us all. Welcome, dear readers and friends, come in. Enter the tavern of higher awareness today, this very moment. The door is wide open. Drums and strings and flutes are playing. The cupbearer is pouring freely. No limits exist on either thirst or wine. Come drink with us. Feel the music vibrate in your heart, and let the wine of spirit flow through your soul. Let us praise the winemaker and become drunk together. Let us unite. Welcome, friends, to the tavern. Welcome to the world of Haféz.

A New World

Let's offer flowers, pour a cup of libation,
split open the skies and start anew on creation.

If the forces of grief invade our lovers' veins,
cupbearer and I will wash away this temptation.

With rose water we'll mellow crimson wine's bitter cup;
we'll sugar the fire to sweeten smoke's emanation.

Take this fine lyre, musician, strike up a love song;
let's dance, sing all night, go wild in celebration.

As dust, O West Wind, let us rise to the Heavens,
floating free in Creator's glow of elation.

If mind desires to return while heart cries to stay,
here's a quarrel for love's deliberation.

Alas, these words and songs go for naught in this land;
come, Haféz, let's create a new generation.

One Soul Standing Guard

by Haleh Pourafzal

I come from the land where the first expression of divine unity was born. Taking shape as an airborne arrow of wisdom originating in ancient Sumeria, this openhearted yearning pierced the heart of the prophet Zarathustra more than three thousand seven hundred years ago, sped on to Persepolis in 500 B.C.E., and then landed in Iran's southern city of Shiraz nearly seven hundred years ago.

In Shiraz, this arrow was glimpsed and grasped by a child with wondrous eyes and a mind as sharp as the arrowhead, a mentality capable of penetrating the heart of all matters and finding there the spirit of life. This child, whom we now call Haféz, tuned in to the ancient voices carried forward on the west wind of his own ancestry and learned the stories of old Persia, the music of Mesopotamia, the philosophy of Plato. Then he imprinted his own poems like fingerprints on the arrow of wisdom, that they might endure and evolve in ages to come.

The arrow traveled on through time and space, flashing its inspiration for millions. Then, six hundred years after Haféz, it struck in the city of Tehran and pierced the heart of a young girl who yearned for a song deeper than any other she had ever heard. I was this girl, and the person who brought Haféz's voice to my soul was my father. For years, I watched and listened as he whispered the words of the poet while carrying out the everyday actions of his life. Whether shaving in the early morning or sitting quietly in the evening, he seemed always to murmur the soft tones of Haféz.

At times he also recited the poetry aloud. In a bass voice that shook from the vibrations of deep-seated feelings held too long in his powerful psyche, he would project Haféz's poetry with profound passion as a cry for understanding and a call to wakefulness, feelings I would embody for the rest of my life. I believe my father read Haféz to enlighten his own spirit, as though the poet were the only soul capable of comprehending the intimate turns of his complex mind, willing to give him the benefit of the doubt. My father's personal bond with Haféz became a prelude to my own intimacy with the poet. Later, my uncle also read Haféz to me, and our extended family of poetry lovers became the circle within which I nurtured a deepening relationship with Haféz.

My affinity for the poet became stronger through annual visits to Shiraz during childhood and adolescent years. Every spring, in celebration of the Iranian New Year (*Norouz*), our family would gather at my aunt and uncle's house in Shiraz. One of our favorite activities during these gatherings was a tour of Haféz's mausoleum, Hafézieh, located in Mosalla, a beautiful garden on the periphery of the city. In the middle of a simple structure of dome and columns that appeared majestic to my eyes, I shared secrets with Haféz. I would tell him about problems with parents and boyfriends and schools. And I sought his advice by opening a copy of the *Divan*, the collection of his poems, which lay by his tomb.

Haféz's response was always to the point and relevant. I felt I was heard, cared for, and embraced by a warm soul who understood my deepest feelings, could see the darkest spots of my soul, skipped over them without judgment, and then spoke to the center of my being, which could hear and feel beyond the cluttered confusion of my thoughts. That is how Haféz became my trusted friend.

One of my fondest memories of the visits to Hafézieh was during the widely celebrated two-thousand-five-hundredth anniversary of the Persian Empire in 1971. It was a beautiful night, and stars abounded in lovely Shiraz. Hafézieh was the site of a performance by Ravi Shankar, the renowned Indian sitar player. Shankar's hypnotic music filled the dome of the mausoleum, and the soft wind transported the graceful sound to my ears in a magical trajectory that has sustained its grounding power in my soul through time. That night, Haféz's poetry took on the added dimension of music to my ear. Later, I discovered through reading that my favorite poet was also a master of music, knowledgeable in both its art and its science.

Among memories of Haféz's home, another image formed very clearly in my early years. During our annual trips to Shiraz, in addition to Hafézieh, I would also visit the ruins of Persepolis. Here was the lofty palace and site of the capital of the Persian Empire of Cyrus the Great. Cyrus came to power in 550 B.C.E. and founded a dynasty that governed an area of forty-eight countries, extending from the Mediterranean Sea to Central Asia and from the Black Sea to Arabia. Although most of Persepolis was destroyed by Alexander the Great in 331 B.C.E., even the ruins evoked the majestic image of ancient Persia. I imagined victorious soldiers wearing impenetrable battle armor, mounted on strong horses and riding up hundreds of short steps to reach the triumphant king, who would thank them for their courage and engage them in celebration.

The connection between Persepolis and Haféz became clear to me in later years when I discovered that much of Haféz's poetry recalls the glory of Iran's past. That was when we Iranians first embraced the vision of one God and translated it directly into the creation of a unified society based on democratic principles, egalitarian ownership, international trade, and innovative agricultural and water management. This vision was the source of the clear voice of unity and quintessential justice that emanates with exceptional power and clarity from Haféz. Amid the abundant symbolism and lyrical liveliness of the poet's verses, unity and justice have emerged for me as the gold of Haféz's ingenious and cunning poetic alchemy. This is the message that has mesmerized my soul, brought me ever closer to Haféz, and compels me to write this book.

As a human being, a woman, a multicultural citizen of the world, I feel a compelling drive to bring to you the words and wisdom of my dear friend Haféz. And it is a special privilege to do this work with two very special men: my father and my life companion business partner. One is the man whose passionate soul carried the voice of Haféz to my psyche. The other is the man who grounded me deeply into my adopted home, America, by teaching me the wisdom of this land's Aztec and Mayan ancestries. Together we create the eye of a triangle that opens wide to offer our vision of Haféz to twenty-first-century humanity.

The arrow that began its journey in ancient Persia, collected the fingerprints of wisdom in Shiraz, and pierced the consciousness of my childhood in Tehran now has landed in America. From this point of awareness and expression, it looks to the future and asks the question: What is Haféz's message to humanity as we evolve through the Information Age and strive for deeper meaning in our life and work?

I turn to Haféz now because this is a rocky time in humanity's history and I am one with the rest of the Earth, because the crossroads of progress and regression where we stand at this juncture demands sobriety and confidence, and because we can use another shining ray of light to warm our hearts and illumine the way. I know that whenever my own pathway has demanded such tools, I have asked for and received them from Haféz. His soul always has stood guard within my being. And now I introduce him to you.

Through Haféz, I have learned that life is a pathway of service and that service means transcendence of self through fully embracing the world. Through him, I have learned to both absorb and transform my own memories of experiences such as these:

- A dark street in central Tehran. I was seven years old, holding my pregnant mother's hand. High-pitched shouts of two men pierced the summer night. Goose bumps rose on my thin skin. I turned my head. Knives, blood, one man lying on the ground, a few others watching. "He deserved it," a trembling woman screamed. An image of hatred projected on my childhood's psyche.
- A winter night near Harvard Square in Cambridge, Massachusetts. An Iranian couple's sleep was disrupted by the crash of shattering window glass. From down the hallway, I heard the newborn baby girl cry out. A rock lay in the middle of the tiny, sparse living room, surrounded by a hundred slivers of glass. "Give our hostages back," angry teenage voices shouted from the darkness of the night outside.
- A spring afternoon, and a grandmother joined the crowd of demonstrators in southern Tehran. Colorful placards raised high, fists clenched in the soft air. Iron will and anger in massive supply. The men in front, the women behind. Black veils, dark beards, grinding teeth. Bewildered children lending their shiny eyes to the scene. On television, I watched the strange enchantment mingle with slogans. "Death to America," one hundred bullhorns echoed in unison.

Whenever scenes such as these revived in my mind, I would dream of Haféz's kind face and hear his gentle, yet witty and sober voice. His poems would call me to the reality of light and shadow and the duality within the single source of creation. He would remind me, with his uniquely clever and soothing verses, that the wisdom of this duality resides in the very fact that it keeps us on our toes and makes us responsible for how we see things and how we act in the world; that every moment, we have the power to choose one thing over another, but that seemingly bad choices are also pathways for learning and growth. After all, Haféz would say, we are here for only a short while.

Earth has spun around the sun many times since my remembered scenes of violence between the Iranian and American peoples implanted themselves on humanity's psyche. Sometimes we have allowed friendship in; sometimes we've opted for intolerance. But no matter our choice, reality keeps haunting us like those angry, shrieking voices in my childhood on that summer night long ago.

Anger is the other side of fear—fear of others who do not match our expectations of normality, fear of those who reflect the parts of ourselves that beg for attention and integration, fear that separating to discover our uniqueness will not lead to reunion. But fear has a double too: fearlessness, that deep confidence in the innate wisdom of humankind to perpetuate a vision of oneness that will stand tall amidst fragmentation. It is high time that we, sisters and brothers in this short journey on Earth, make a quantum leap toward fearlessness. Somehow, our perceptions of separation must melt away like winter snow in early spring. One day, we will see with the clarity of still water that all our anger and determination to pull apart from each other are but the shadow of our passion for unity and peace.

As I ponder the separation of my own parts, reflecting the peoples of Iran and America, of the East and the West, I see a very simple pathway toward unity: I give you my most precious prize— my best friend, Haféz. He can help us walk more skillfully the razor's edge between integration and alienation. He can inspire us with the lucidity, depth, and beauty of his poetry to put forth a vision of the future based on what every one of us yearns for: community, justice, creativity, productivity, fulfillment, and prosperity. As we prepare for the future, we can benefit by recalling the wise voices of our past.

As customary in the world of business, I play the role of the broker, the bridge builder. I introduce you to Haféz, and the two of you can decide how to proceed. As we come to meet with you, Haféz, as usual, whispers in my ears that I must put my words of friendship into action. So I open his book of poems, seeking his guidance for this book. This verse comes to you and me:

> *Hatred and hypocrisy close the heart, Haféz,*
> *so I choose rendi, path of the libertine-love.*

Rendi, as we will explain later, is Hafez's pathway to unity. It is the way of the *rend,* the person who both seeks unity and models it in the search process. This is the person of the twenty-first century. A critical mass of rends can turn the tides of confusion and propel humanity into an era of constructive imagination and action in unifying and synchronizing our collective transformation.

This is Haféz's message to every member of the human family. And this is a book to the forward-looking visionary movement everywhere from the soil of my extended homeland, America. As we join hands and hearts to celebrate humanity's common bond and our unity with the rest of creation, Haféz speaks to us all.

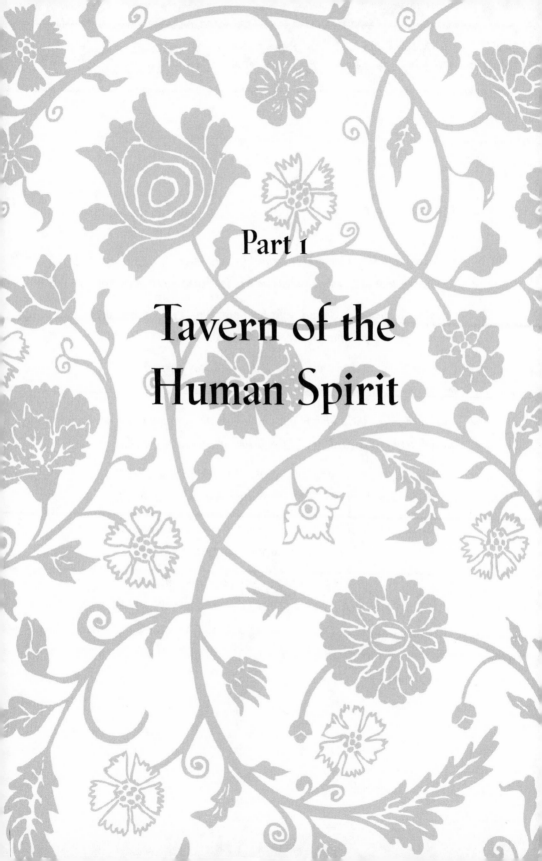

Part 1

Tavern of the
Human Spirit

The Secret

I need a drink, wine maiden, that cup with grape stain lined,
for love that once seemed pleasing has burdened down my mind.

Ah smell how West Wind wafts her musk through the tavern door;
now feel our pumping hearts beat fast, watch our fears unwind.

Why would we who visit love think we'd stay forever?
We know the yearn to wander will always lovers find.

So we asked the Elder: What law makes love bring pain?
Sobriety, he laughed, you'll feel better when you're wined.

Your plight cannot be aided by that dull fear to risk
the toss and turn of love's dark storm upon the ocean blind.

See clear in all these gathered friends who still hold you dear
love's secret is that you must love without desires that bind.

Haféz, enjoy the one you love, drink deep and embrace;
seek not with her to please your world, just give love and be kind.

Philosopher of Love

Our truest position is this corner bench of the tavern;
may she who built this house be raised up by Creator.

Haféz inspires the best within us. Out of his verses burst volup-
tuous images of the vanished world of medieval Persia, the tears of
lovers separated in the night, the subtle shivering of a nightingale's
call, the incessant passing of seasons, and the sadness and longing
for that which we know will complete us but which we cannot
see. Haféz is a mystic philosopher and futuristic counselor, a musi-
cal poet of desires, pains, and fears. He is a guide in our search for
life's essence—for God—and he provides us fuel for thinking our
most exultant thoughts in every moment. His artistry challenges
us, above all, to live the best way we can, a way that is free, clear,
and powerful.

Perhaps this challenge accounts for the world's long fascina-
tion with this Persian poet. We want to understand what our best
is, to aspire to our highest possibilities in search of revelation. We
struggle to comprehend genius, to experience its feeling, to ex-
amine its parts in the hope that they will add up to the whole.
Sublime artistry opens our hearts, and our minds strive to keep

pace by evaluating the art form itself, be it an exquisitely woven carpet or a poem that illumines the universe.

Occasionally, one among us designs and executes a finely crafted carpet of lustrous beauty whose threads of thought and feeling weave such an expansive inner-world kaleidoscope that even our minds surrender in awe and open to the same unified perceptions as our hearts. To spread this carpet of beauty across humanity's threshold as a passageway into a multidimensional world of spontaneous understanding and feeling is to practice creativity on its most encompassing and engaging plane.

Such is the poetic power of Haféz. Through his unmatched command of the Farsi language's sweeping scope of expression, he articulated a unique and compelling vision of humanity's journey. He chronicled the giants of history who passed through Persia and the passions of humanity that pass through all of us. He exposed the cutting-edge spiritual and intellectual visions of his time to an eye of fierce intelligence under a high-powered microscope of absolutely ruthless love. No one, least of all the poet himself, escaped the gaze of his all-consuming artistry, which peered without pity through every surface appearance until only truth remained.

In the poem that opens this chapter, which is also the poem that appears first in most editions of the *Divan*, Haféz seeks the answer to why love, as we humans experience it, is accompanied by pain. He consults the Elder, a being we encounter often in the poet's work as his inner voice, his source of spiritual guidance. In Haféz's terminology, the phrase for the Elder is Pir-e-Moghan, an evolved human being, a sage who first appeared in Persian spirituality in the Mazda religious tradition about the time that Zarathustra was founding Zoroastrianism.

> *So we asked the Elder: What law makes love bring pain?*
> *Sobriety, he laughed, you'll feel better when you're wined.*

Get out of your mind, says the Elder, and into your heart. Don't be afraid to feel. Be willing to take a chance.

> *Your plight cannot be aided by that dull fear to risk*
> *the toss and turn of love's dark storm upon the ocean*
>   *blind.*

Then the secret is revealed:

> *See clear in all these gathered friends who still hold you dear*
> *love's secret is that you must love without desires that bind.*

And finally, the Elder opens the way for more love:

> *Haféz, enjoy the one you love, drink deep and embrace;*
> *seek not with her to please your world, just give love and*
>   *be kind.*

This unselfish generosity in love stands as an essential pillar of Haféz's worldview. Another pillar is absolute truth and integrity in all public and private considerations. He pointed out the hypocrisy of many public figures of his time, and for this he was hated as well as loved. Over centuries, his tomb in his home city of Shiraz has been the scene of both desecration and celebration. Today, more than six hundred years after his passing, the rebuilt mausoleum stands as a monument to his artistry, and more books have been written about him than about any other Persian person. The poet's words of truth have survived.

From his own writing, we extract the image of Haféz as an accomplished, clever, humorous man who reveled in beauty, reviled orthodoxy, and survived adversity. His outlook on life may have been formed quite early. It is said that he was born in the *shayyadan* neighborhood in Shiraz, a rough locale known as the home turf of a community of spiritual charlatans, practitioners of a blend of fundamentalist religion, metaphysics, and superstition. Ironically, it may have been the youngster's firsthand experience with this subculture that ultimately helped him form a worldview that stood uncompromisingly against such practices.

Historians place Haféz's birth around the year 1320 and his death at about 1388 to 1390. Born Shams-ud-Din Mohammad, the young poet adopted the pen name "Haféz," which can be translated literally as "the memorizer." Legend says that the name refers to his having memorized the Koran during his youth. In Iran, he also is called Lessan-ul-Gheib, an Arabic name meaning "Tongue of the Unseen."

In the midst of a flourishing culture that considered poetry a sublime art, Haféz wrote with an unprecedented range of expression that enriched the five-hundred-year lineage of such renowned Persian poets as the blind harpist Rudaki, Ferdowsi, Khayyam, Sanaï, Farid-ud-Din Attar, Nézami, Rumi, and Saadi. His work seems to embody the best attributes of his predecessors, and yet the content is uniquely his own, a soaring composite orchestrated by a master's pen. Persian readers love Haféz because they hear a symphony in his poems—a multifaceted work of strings and flutes and drums, their passionate vibrations blended into an extraordinary whole.

Haféz's more than five hundred surviving poems are estimated to represent about 10 percent of his total work. The rest apparently was destroyed by civil authorities displeased by the content of his verses. Most of his surviving poems have been collected in the *Divan,* a book assembled after his death and utilized by modern Persians as a divination tool. In a land of great poets and universally proclaimed mystics, it is the work of Haféz that remains relevant as daily guidance because he writes not only on spirituality but also on social, political, and economic concerns. To Haféz, more than any other Persian poet, the practicality of living well was as important as the ecstasy of visionary states. He was a mystic, but he was also a man of the world, and his vision embraced both realities.

Although today's Sufis often claim him as one of their early scribes, Haféz's writing aimed taunts and barbs at both the Moslem and Sufi fundamentalists of his day. Apparently a court poet during much of his composing life, he laced his poems with social commentary. He also wrote of the trials of everyday life and of having endured the death of a son. People continue to love and trust and commune with Haféz because his spirituality is that of all humanity, not of any isolated groups or secret traditions.

Haféz embraced the Persian lexicon, in which wine represents enlightenment, truth, grace, knowledge—the essence flowing from God. The source of all is called the winemaker; the teacher is the cupbearer; the place of learning is the tavern. Intoxication from such wine induces direct perception of existence at its universal source. To bring the wisdom of that lofty perception to our material world as properly focused love and work is the challenge of life, the purpose of sobriety, and the goal of humanity's quest.

Through the imagery of the beloved as the focus of one's love and adoration, another well-established element of Persian poetry, Haféz revives in our minds the hidden form of a primordial love-projecting and justice-seeking essence. The tiny crevice in the beloved's chin is the well of shadows, the place where we become lost only to find ourselves again. The mole slightly above the beloved's ruby lips is the signpost for discovering the source of all creation. The kisses from those lips are the funnels through which we receive the intoxicating power of the wine of awareness, the elixir of life. The long black hair that hangs or spreads to show its endless waves is the landscape of the infinite tosses and turns of life and the nightlike darkness of the heart's silence. And the beloved's seductive smile serves as invitation to the spiritual path. Everything starts here, when we see that smile and decide to respond. But beware of what is in store, Haféz laughs; it is not as easy as it seems.

For Haféz, always in search of rapture with the beloved, Shiraz was a shining tavern of awareness in which he drank the wine of spirit and then sang its tales to the world as no one before or since:

Sweet Shiraz—gorgeous city of worldly wonder rare;
may your spirit never wander, this is my blessing prayer.

Haféz passed most of his seventy years of life in this city of light and sound and sensuality. At the time, Persians swore that no other place in the world matched the beauty of the gardens, mosques, and bazaars of Shiraz. The dominant Islamic society synthesized

the surviving elements of ancient Persia with the best of the im-
ported Arab, Hellenistic, Christian, Jewish, Hermetic, and Indian
cultures. Here was the Middle East's artistic hub, home of the
country's most famous dancing schools and dancers, a society of
burgeoning wealth, a gathering place for learned teachers and sa-
cred writings of the great spiritual traditions, and a city of worldly
pleasures to seduce the imagination. Undoubtedly, Haféz cast his
eye on many types of delights:

> *Ruby lips and dark eyes everywhere in Shiraz,*
> *but I'm a poor craftsman and cannot afford.*
>
> *All these languishing eyes I see here in Shiraz,*
> *but mellow I am with just wine and my lord.*
>
> *Beauties short beauties tall strolling throughout Shiraz;*
> *for them, were I wealthy, I'd offer my hoard.*

This poem, of course, suggests that Haféz's perception of love
includes the physical aspects as well as the spiritual. From the big
picture presented by his entire body of work, we are left with the
delightful confirmation that Haféz the philosopher envisioned love
as a condition of absolute unity. He was not interested in excluding
any aspect of reality from its appropriate place in the scheme of
humanity. In fact, the love in Haféz's poetry becomes such an ex-
pansive concept that it extends to our most basic essence. Like the
energy known as *chi* in Chinese philosophy and the force of breath
called *prana* in Sanskrit, Haféz's love emerges as the primal element
of all existence. The poet extended his love to the river Roknabad
as well, seeing it as the veins and its water as the blood of Shiraz:

> *Cupbearer, pour all that remains of the wine;*
> *Paradise has no Roknabad or Mosalla garden.*

Throughout the city, painters created their already famous
Persian miniatures with incredibly delicate brushes. Artisans ex-
celled in carpet weaving, metalwork, and ceramics. Roses and
grapes and nightingales abounded. A light breeze blew much of
the time, cooling the otherwise arid climate. Desert dwellers jour-

neyed into Shiraz to raise their tents in comfort amid the shade of towering cypress trees on the city's outskirts. All this crafted a lovely, unified picture in the poet's imagination.

While Haféz chronicled the beauty of his city throughout his decades of writing verse, he also was a writer who revealed the two sides of every story. This actually was a dark time in Persian history: an embattled era of high political intrigue, deadly treachery, and warring sultans. The poet spent many years dealing with public adversaries ranging from local mullahs to Mongol invaders, and he apparently retained his position at court through several regime changes—some of them violent. A master of paradoxical maneuvers in both verse and life, Haféz survived the turmoil of his times—and so did his beloved Shiraz.

That the poet's work remains relevant today is a product of his capacity to perceive events beyond the limitations of space and time. Camel caravans on the Silk Road from China brought in international trade and an awareness of foreign cultures, and he recognized past and future in the present of his city. The worries of Shiraz included ambitious politicians armed with the latest war machinery, robbers on the roads, religious intolerance, land use reforms, race relations, environmental abuses that encouraged famine, and an unfair system of taxation.

Although he spent almost all his life in Shiraz, Haféz painted a universal vision of his local world. Even if he could have accessed world news on a fourteenth-century "Internet," the paradoxical nature of his commentary on humanity and its pursuits probably would not have changed. In Europe, the Crusades had ended, and the Inquisition, witch-burning, and the black death of bubonic plague raged. The full flowering of the Renaissance was still a century away. In Mexico, the Aztec Empire was taking control of neighboring peoples, unaware that Europeans were dreaming of sailing ships and great voyages that would lead to the Spanish Conquest. But there was also great art in the world. Dante Alighieri died in Italy near the time of the birth of Haféz in Persia, about twenty years before Geoffrey Chaucer was born in England. The No drama of Japan was blending music, song, dance, and poetry into public performance as no previous theater form had done. In India, the stringed sitar and the tabla drum recently had been invented. These and derivative instruments would become traditional accompaniment, along with the flute, for the recitation of Persian poetry, creating music that continues to this day for Haféz's tavern of the spirit.

Unlimited by the boundaries of Shiraz or the happenings of his century, Haféz propelled his own message forward through time. His words are known not only in his homeland but also throughout the Middle East, Asia, and Europe. More than two hundred years ago, British scholars began translating his verse into English. The thoughts Haféz formulated in his own divine intoxication and sent forth through lines of rhyme still speak as meaningfully as ever to those of us living on the cusp of the twenty-first century:

> For one or two moments your precious seeing exists;
> discern heart's true path while your eyes are open.

We—the writers of this book—are a Persian woman and an American man. As such, we embrace perspectives both female and male as well as Eastern and Western, and we hear with equal clarity this message of Haféz. Both we as writers and you as readers are the beneficiaries of this message. All of us, representing myriad perspectives, are the ones to whom the poet speaks—we modern women and men who must meet and greet the twenty-first century with its unimaginable agenda of pressures and possibilities and perplexities. We alone must hold our souls together amid the expanding demands of laboring and living and loving and laughing, we who are in search of inner meaning and outer functioning and who are alive in a world of six billion humans breathing in a nurturing but restrictive atmosphere on a minuscule planet in a tiny solar system of an ancient galaxy of an expanding universe. All of us can access and use the wisdom of Haféz. He is here, just as he has been for more than six hundred years—we simply haven't heard him quite clearly. Perhaps it is because we have been listening for a symphony of Eastern music, while the poet himself created a masterpiece thoroughly adaptable to a Western orchestra. But now, perhaps, we are learning to listen.

Haféz is relevant to the spiritual movement of today because he traveled a mystical path that addresses the one central question of any mystic: How do I find my unique way of self-actualization? Haféz's first entry point to the mystical path was the same as that of any other seeker of spiritual growth: a deep desire for the well of creativity within. In his case, this was poetry. He pursued this yearning with undivided focus, hard work, and perseverance. He reached his well and spent the rest of his life drinking from its fountain with an astonishing balance of reverence and realism that has resulted in the sustainability of his poetry. This balance—this element of sustainability that characterized Haféz's individualized pathway to mastery—came about through four stages of growth.

The poet's first window to mysticism was religion. He mastered the Koran. But, as still happens today, Haféz apparently found organized religion too narrow and was repelled by its fundamentalist tendencies. The poet's continual search to reach beyond the limits of ordinary thought led him to Sufism, his second step. He drank from that well too, as he sought to quench his thirst for a more expanded horizon of thought and imagination. But while participating in the heartbeat of the esoteric Sufi philosophy, Haféz's unwavering focus on reaching enlightenment through a unique pathway rejected the fundamentalist tendencies of Sufi practitioners as well. Instead, he kept reaching further into the freer territories of his culture's ancient past. His third stage of spiritual development took him all the way back to the period of Zoroastrianism, not for rituals and prescribed solutions, but for the power of innovation.

Finally, when he began to perceive the approach of his own death, he identified his kindred spirit not as a mullah, a Sufi master, or a Zoroastrian elder, but rather as the wild deer—an animal guide who had already gone over to the other side. Haféz passed through this world free from the weight of attachment and went on to the next in the same way. The genius of his poetry, which touches the hearts of readers, rests in the simple quality of balance through nonattachment: Take from everything that captures your imagination, stop and touch any flower that attracts you, and drink from the well of knowledge and wisdom. But don't exhaust either yourself or the world through attachments and indulgence.

Naturally, the details of each person's mystic path will vary. Instead of the Koran, there may be the Bible; instead of Sufism, there may be Zen; instead of Zoroastrianism, there may be Goddess paganism. But the essential thread of the spiritual journey remains the same today as it was in Haféz's life—we each have to find our own way. Haféz's poetry is an inspiration to those who want to tap into the intricacies of this simple truth. His philosophy speaks with a rare combination of eloquence and beauty to the challenges of contemporary lives. The poetic form through which he expresses his philosophy and the characteristics of his unique mystical path provide inspiration to spiritual seekers and poetry lovers, who find an illuminating friend in this Persian scribe.

That Haféz is not better known to the Western public is owing, international scholars speculate, to the inherent limitations of translation. Most early translated works featured poems selected for their imagery and beauty or for such topics as Haféz's intense denunciation of the religious hypocrisy of his times. Those efforts cast Haféz into a role on the periphery of Western literary thought as a genius whose range of artistry seems to be cut off from non-Persian perception by his sophisticated but nontranslatable mastery of Farsi.

In recent years, however, a new perspective is emerging, the same perspective that inspired UNESCO to create the Haféz Conference in Paris and to designate 1988 as the "Year of Haféz." The reason the poet is not better understood in the West, this viewpoint states, is that translators have not previously interpreted the main thrust of his writing in terms of either a wide-ranging, futuristic thought process with universal applications or the broad context of ancient wisdom precepts that Aldous Huxley called the "perennial philosophy"—the rudimentary spiritual perception that embraces a divine reality and has informed all the world's major spiritual traditions.

The presence of ancient wisdom precepts is obvious in many references throughout Haféz's verses, such as Pir-e-Moghan, the Elder or evolved human who dates back to Zarathustra's time. In addition, Haféz lived in Persia at a time when the world's great scientific and philosophical writings were readily available, and his poetry offers testimony both subtle and obvious that he was thoroughly schooled in the diverse disciplines of his day. Not only was he a consummate metaphysical philosopher in the grand tradition dating back to Plato, he was also keenly aware of the other side of intoxication, the sobering scientific observation of objective reality. It is this combination of ancient roots and scientific perspective that projects Haféz's thinking into our own time as valid observation and counsel.

As we add the role of mystic philosopher to his previous status as poet of genius, Haféz instantly assumes a prominence in philosophical thought on the level of the ancient writers of China, Greece, and India as well as his own Persian homeland. Our emerging image of Haféz is that of a visionary sage whose teachings on awareness have transcended the ages through the vehicle of his poetry, a vehicle that has endured because it is brilliantly constructed in the highest artistic styles of his time and culture.

To create a context in the lineage of the perennial philosophy in which to consider Haféz as mystic philosopher, we must start with the idea that sometime in the dawn of thought, the eye of our species peered into a pool of clear water and perceived that every image projects a reflection. Cogitating on that phenomenon, the mind of humankind formulated, perhaps slowly but surely, the principle of duality: the day and night of the sky, the birth and death of creatures, the inner and outer concerns of living, and, eventually, the two sides to every question.

Our mythologies and philosophies of existence on this spinning planet Earth have been concerned primarily with the observation and reconciliation of these two most obvious aspects of our being. Our creation stories abound around the personification of opposing pairs, such as Eden's Cain and Abel, Rome's Romulus and Remus, and the ancient Mayans' Hero Twins. These

stories explain that we are the mysterious result of yin and yang—
or Ahura and Ahriman, in the ancient Persian context—coming
together and splitting apart, time after time. How these opposing
forces create life is the mystery we all share and pursue. That they
interact so dynamically and efficiently is evidence of an extreme
level of synergistic competence.

Of all world philosophers that we remember, few have pre-
sented to humanity as lucid or as inspired an account of how to
embrace this paradox as Haféz. In essence, he tells us to trust the
wondrous power of that guiding force of existence to which we
all belong and in which we all participate. He tells us to trust love.
But he also tells us, in his very next breath, to temper that trust
with the highest possible application of human intelligence. For
Haféz, this paradoxically tempered trust is the answer to paradox
itself. He cautions:

> *Seek not faithfulness from our wobbly world;*
> *this witch is false bride to a thousand grooms.*

And again:

> *Guard well your soul against worldly seductions;*
> *this witch blinks deceit and disappears slyly.*

And one more time:

> *The bride of the world is awesomely lovely;*
> *but beware, she seeks no binding marriage.*

In other words, we must know ourselves so well that we do not
rely on the outer world for our meaning and our survival. We
must respond to every challenge with a spontaneous blend of in-
stinct and thought. Life is full of surprising challenges moment
after moment, and the last thing we need is a fundamentalist ap-
proach that limits our capacity to envision new possibilities.

Were we to paraphrase Haféz in English, the condensed wis-
dom of the poet's writings would read something like this:

• If you yearn for inner peace and want to know love, if you wish to be a spiritual seeker like me, you can search for your personal treasure through ecstatic intoxication.

- I give you my thoughts at the entrance to this tavern of intoxication. Taste them as a first sip of spiritual wine.
- This pathway to inner peace is at odds with two deadly enemies: hypocrisy and profanity. Hypocrisy is the way of established order as it seeks to protect and prolong itself at all costs. Profanity is the mindless waste of those who react destructively to established order.
- At the same time, ecstasy demands that you seek ultimate pleasure. But be aware. If the pleasure embodies either hypocrisy or profanity, you will be at war with yourself.
- The weapons for this war and the openings to this pleasure are all within you. You must find them in your intoxication and then use them in the material world. Such application requires constant attunement with your inner core, acting on direct instinct, and deep laughter that unties the knots of emotion.
- If you are truly journeying to love, your final goal must be only one thing: perceiving and expressing truth.

These ideas come alive with remarkable clarity throughout the poet's body of work. Whether writing about Shiraz's beautiful river Roknabad or calling for the cupbearer to pour more wine for his friends in the tavern, Haféz the sage is always present in Haféz the poet. While the poet constructs delightful musical rhythms, the sage depicts the pathway of spiritual pursuits.

Although the language of this philosophy addresses the individual seeker, Haféz speaks just as effectively to entire cultures. He invites absolutely everyone into the tavern. Extending these ideas to our immensely powerful, yet highly impersonal Information Age, we discover such modern and timely advice as this:

- All limitations of mind and relationships exist to be extended.
- The harshness with which we are tempted to deal with one another must be overcome.

- Generosity of spirit and service to all humankind are the most powerful and appropriate motivations for everything.
- And yet, be smart, friends, be very smart. Paradox exists everywhere. There is a subtle but definite difference between, for instance, generosity of service and destructiveness of self-sacrifice. Clear your mind. Don't be fooled by appearances—this is the clever way of Haféz.

To further paraphrase the poet, when you clear your mind, you learn to see the big picture of existence in which duality melts into itself and paradox resolves. This gives you confidence to trust your own perceptions. As you begin to see worldly relationships in new and clearer perspectives, you learn to deal directly and effectively with these relationships. Mastering this direct dealing results in competence in handling your daily affairs. Living every waking and every sleeping moment in this self-empowering condition becomes the purpose of Haféz's pathway.

The poet's philosophy can assist us modern folk as we battle for daily sanity in our computerized, mechanized, impersonalized, yet extremely potent Information Age. In this context, the revelations of Haféz become an ideal source for refocusing our present and future into a simple yet sublime vision. This approach embraces the spiritual forces that inspire us, inform our reasoning, and mold the conduct and outcome of life itself. It acknowledges soul and poetry throughout all aspects of our existence, and it envisions life as a self-organizing entity embracing our inner yearnings as well as our outer requirements. It allows us to extend love to ourselves through words as clear as these:

> *God protects those who walk the true path*
> *from treachery of those who don't care.*
>
> *O heart, live such that if your foot slips,*
> *angels' hands will catch you in prayer.*

He also offers quite specific recommendations for the conduct of our public affairs:

Garden flowers will not stay fresh forever;
remember the poor when you sit in power.

Haféz is an ultimate humanist. Perhaps the simplest summary of his philosophy is that it clearly reflects the Zen Buddhist precepts of gratitude to the past, service to the present, and responsibility to the future. He calls for us to envision ourselves unconditionally as part of the whole of creation. This wisdom of unity is the wine Haféz offers. Enlightenment can be our intoxication. As the poet speaks to each of us in the quiet of mind as well as in the context of all humanity, many around the world already hear his symphony delivered with such lyrical power and conviction that, for them, he stands alone as a seer and scribe whose spirit travels from old Shiraz into the present.

But where, you well may ask, does Haféz stand alone today? Where can we find him? How can the contemporary world in its current need access guidance from this ancient Persian genius? He stands, friends, in the tavern of the human spirit. There he advises us to find ourselves through feeling, to dance ourselves into ecstasy. Holding this book, you well may sense his presence or even his voice whispering quietly within your most private thoughts. That's one way he operates. Now, in our own present, this philosopher of love reaches into our hearts and minds with his every insight and with this invitation:

A mysterious voice whispered just as dawn came:
your spirit fears nothing—drink wine, be the same.

No mysteries can hide from the seeking of youth;
new teachings are calling, old truth is the game.

So I tune up my lyre and I wake up my song,
yearning for ages in this heart and this name.

Let us turn wine to wisdom, violate law's design;
let us yield to the joy of music aflame.

THE SEARCH

Go search for Jam's Cup, cried my heart so vain,
as though from some stranger its truth I'd obtain.

The pearl peering out from its sea-shaped shell
sought vision from souls lost in ocean's domain.

This to my Elder last night I revealed,
praying an answer to the riddle I'd gain.

Lighthearted he listened, then wine cup raised,
revealing a mirror where worlds wax and wane.

When did Wisdom give such a cup? I inquired.
On the day she shaped sky's blue dome, he said sane.

She whose heart holds secrets like buds sealed tight
inscribed images deep in memory's refrain.

Blind to this truth we stroll with God through life,
madly shouting, O God, come to me, soothe my pain.

Our minds raise up worship over clear sight
such as Moses' decree that from idols abstain.

Elder explained crime of friend who was hanged
was speaking such secrets in language too plain.

Truth is, if Gabriel would open our eyes,
Christ's vision can be seen by others again.

O Elder, why does our search never cease?
Jam's Cup, dear Haféz, is your link to friend's chain.

Jamshid's Biluminous Cup

*T*he Cup of Jamshid is Haféz's Holy Grail, a wondrous goblet offering humanity a gleaming glimpse of the liberating potential of existence. As we contemporary seekers accept Haféz's invitation to enter into his tavern of the human spirit, we find there is no cover charge for the music and dancing. But in order to remain and drink deeply of the fine wine—to study, to befriend and comprehend this master of wisdom—a precious fee is demanded. That fee is the immersion of our consciousness into the biluminous mystery that whirls around and throughout the deeper dimensions of the Cup of Jamshid.

Jamshid—often called Jam—is the greatest hero of Persian mythology. Indo-Iranian tradition tells us that he united the ancient kingdom of Persia in an all-but-forgotten time, built monuments and roads, and ruled for hundreds of years. Known as the "good shepherd," he is said to have brought wealth and well-being to his people by advancing agriculture, creating metallurgy, and teaching silk and wool weaving. Like all mortals, however, Jam was subject to making mistakes, and he eventually made some bad choices that cost him his throne. But bad personal choices do not invalidate the power of the soul's potential. Jam's Cup, in the language of Haféz's poetic lineage, is the vessel within which the secret of Earthly powers is concealed. Naturally, we are all searching for it.

Similarly, the quest for the Holy Grail pervades Western mythology. Mysterious powers are attributed to the Grail, often described as the golden cup from which Jesus drank wine at the Last Supper and which also was used to collect drops of his blood at the foot of the cross. The Grail is the symbol of prosperity, the secret of health and wealth. Parsival sought its elusive reality to save King Arthur's realm. The Knights Templars were rumored to have found it during the Crusades in the Holy Land. As with Jam's Cup, the mysteries of the Holy Grail's existence and power endure.

"The Search," the poem about Jam's Cup at the start of this chapter, illustrates Haféz's capacity to interweave mythology and spiritual principles into a poignant teaching about a universal human riddle. Once again, Haféz has approached his Elder voice of guidance for an explanation, this time as to why we tend to seek truth from sources outside ourselves:

> Go search for Jam's Cup, cried my heart so vain,
> as though from some stranger its truth I'd obtain.

Elder explains that Wisdom, on the day she created "sky's blue dome," also gave humanity the means ("wine cup") to see the true nature of existence ("a mirror where worlds wax and wane"). But our thinking minds cannot comprehend the truth that God and wisdom are always with us. The poet also weaves in one of Sufism's most enduring mystical memories:

> Elder explained crime of friend who was hanged
> was speaking such secrets in language too plain.

The "friend who was hanged" was the tenth-century spiritual teacher Hallaj, who was executed by the fundamentalist Moslem regime for saying, "I am the Truth," which was interpreted as meaning "I am God." This was considered a blasphemous statement punishable by death. Hallaj became an honored spiritual figure in succeeding centuries as Iran's progressive spiritual tradition recognized his words as signifying that there is no separation between humanity and God. This type of public statement ("speaking such secrets in language too plain") always poses a threat to an established clergy, since it declares, in effect, that the clergy is not needed to intercede with God on humanity's behalf. It is widely speculated that religious persecution such as that suffered by Hallaj may have been the original motivation for Persian poets to adopt the camouflage of the wine metaphor when creating verse about spirituality that did not celebrate the dominant belief system.

In the final stanza of the poem, Elder explains that we all continue to seek Jam's Cup because it represents insight into Hallaj's meaning as well as connection to his martyrdom:

> *O Elder, why does our search never cease?*
> *Jam's Cup, dear Haféz, is your link to friend's chain.*

In other words, we are driven to search continually for the secret that we already possess God and wisdom within us. But since our minds look out on the world, seeking "vision from souls lost in ocean's domain" rather than looking inward at the wine cup's image, our only salvation is for Gabriel to open our eyes to the same vision seen by Christ—and by Moses and Haféz himself. This is the vision revealed by the Elder's "mirror where worlds wax and wane": that the nature of reality is dynamic and nonstatic and, therefore, brimming over with potential.

This focus on the need to keep our inner and outer worlds in proper perspective runs through Haféz's writing. While we keep on looking for love and knowledge in all the wrong places, he also continues giving us clues about the true nature of Jam's Cup, as in these individual couplets from different poems:

> *Haféz, if we traveled through this world without woe,*
> *Jamshid's Cup you'd not seek, straight to love you'd not go.*

O you, sitting quiet on your tavern bench,
pick up the cup and take your turn as Jamshid.

If you don't want union, then don't seek the vision;
Jam's Cup offers rewards to only the patient.

They will lift off the veil from the Earth and the stars,
those holders and servers of the world-seeing cup.

If you desire true secrets of mystery,
Jam's Cup seeks only a constant lover.

And this verse introduces a concept that literally lights up the poetry of Haféz:

Like Jam, take a sip from both worlds' secrets,
and cup's radiance will bring you awareness.

When we do find the Cup of Jamshid, Haféz suggests, we are embraced by an empowering knowledge that emanates from within the vessel and enlightens the world outside. A visualization exercise illustrates the nature of this enlightenment. Imagine a crystal coin so thin you can see through it. The mystery of human life with all its joys and woes is imprinted on one side, while the flip side projects a burning brilliance of divine inspiration. This porous coin is like the poetry of Haféz. Only a razor's edge separates the mystery and the brilliance.

Now imagine flipping the coin into the air and watching it spin head over tail over head. Since the coin is porous, brilliant light pours out from both sides. As the coin creates its brief orbit, illumination fills the atmosphere. The razor's edge dissolves from vision, and you lose track of the distinction between mystery and meaning. If you close your eyes just before the coin completes its flight, the image of its glowing orbit imprints on your inner vision and remains there for many seconds. Holding your eyes tightly shut, you marvel that the glow remains visible far longer in inner darkness than if you had left your eyes open.

This is the principle of "biluminosity," or *"tabalvor-e mozaaf,"* a Farsi phrase originated by Abdol-Hossein Pourafzal, this book's literary consultant. Biluminosity is the particular genius embodied in the writings of Haféz, the process of simultaneous enlightenment from two sources, both from personal involvement in the human mystery and from direct perception of divine inspiration. Biluminosity embraces humanity's initial perception of duality and purposefully projects a balanced world of unity.

This concept is an expansion of a Persian literary tool called *iham,* a technique of comparison involving wordplay, sound association, and double entendre, keeping the reader in doubt as to the "right" meaning of the word. Biluminosity removes the burden of choice and invites the reader to enter a more empowering dimension of iham that embraces the quality of amphibians (another Farsi translation of iham is "amphibiology")—beings capable of living equally well in two radically different environments. As a result, the reader is freed from the obsession to find the "right answer" through speculation and instead can concentrate on enjoying nuances and being awed by how the slightest shift in perception creates a new meaning. Through the pedagogy of biluminosity, the reader has the opportunity to develop the qualities of a graceful dancer. This is a powerful tool for adjusting effectively in a world that is unfolding through increasingly sharp contrasts.

Biluminosity can be described as similar to the experience of admiring an exquisitely colored Persian carpet. Depending on where you stand, either off the carpet or at any point on it, the light strikes the threads at different angles, and you see different hues than from any other angle. No matter what color you see, you know that another shade of that color will appear whenever you move to another position. By seeing from wherever you stand, you are participating in the unity of the creative artistry of the carpet. From the perspective of Haféz as the composer of poetry, biluminosity allows two different points of view to shed light upon each other. Without darkness, light cannot be distinguished. Without light, darkness is formless and meaningless.

The nineteenth-century German philosopher Nietzsche, like his countryman Goethe, loved the poetry of Haféz, which he read in an early German translation. Acknowledgment of the unifying quality of biluminosity emerges in this passage from Nietzsche addressed to Haféz:

> The tavern that you have built is larger than any other house. Not everyone is capable of drinking the wine you have prepared. The winged spirit of God is your guest there. You are all: the tavern, the wine, the winged spirit. Eternally you go to your inner self; eternally you come out. . . .
>
> Only the most enlightened of beings can benefit from the deepest human joys because within such beings resides a unique force of freedom and rapture. Their awareness rests in the house of spirit and their soul mates with their awareness, meaning that which is discovered through awareness emanates from their soul and that which shines in the soul is known with awareness. This unity of spirit and mind is the legacy of Haféz.[9]

Biluminosity provides a convenient window for viewing two elements of literary power that distinguish Haféz: first, the voice of wisdom that speaks through his every poem, and, second, an invisible power that propels his message through the ages and into the present. From the poet's point of view, these are his personal benefits from his own discovery of Jam's Cup. Both elements have been gleaming in Haféz's writing for more than six centuries through an endless flow of elusive, enticing teachings cleverly imbedded in virtually every two-line passage.

Quite often, this brilliance is conveyed by a voice that spirals like a serpent threading itself out of a timeless void through Haféz and into his readers. Typical of the final couplets of the poems in the *Divan* is this passage, addressed directly to the poet:

Hafez, one heart hears the enchanted song that you sing;
if your listener is wise that song in the heart grows.

Imbued with wisdom and wit, this voice of guidance speaks as
an entity apart from the poet, criticizing and teasing. Changing
moods with each poem, the voice guides, chides, soothes, de-
mands, reflects, and explains. For instance, this teasing for being
too cerebral in the search for love:

Hafez, you plotted and planned and did your best;
too bad, your wild-hearted love paid you no heed.

Sometimes the poet is held up to ridicule by the voice, as in
this reflective warning that suggests a series of double meanings
for several terms:

My friend, keep your space from tavern's mean street;
Hafez, watching stars, lost sight of that need.

The couplet leaves us asking what precise meanings the poet has
ascribed to "tavern," "mean street," "watching stars," "lost sight,"
and "that need." Is he advising us to keep away from barrooms, as
Hafez failed to do, or is he warning against immersing ourselves
too deeply into spiritual pursuits? Or, more likely, is he saying
both? Or perhaps it's not even a warning. The reader is left in
doubt and therefore alert and inquiring. This state of always being
on one's mental toes—always wondering, yet maintaining integ-
rity of perception—is Hafez's own condition and one that he
generously transfers to his readers as an unassuming teacher and
compassionate friend.

The two levels of meaning of biluminosity grow out of Hafez's
unmistakable presence as well as his personal detachment from
the poems' messages. The reader is free to examine every thought
from the perspectives of both wise teacher and humble spiritual
seeker. As a result, Hafez the poet never places himself in the posi-
tion of preaching to his reader about what to do or not to do.
Instead, biluminosity's second voice shows up to expound on a
lesson for both poet and reader.

This is a superb illustration of the artistic axiom that to suggest is to create. Haféz has molded an ideal vehicle for transporting his wisdom observations through time, identifying himself clearly as the creator of each artistically polished poem while also communicating profound insights for readers clever enough to discern the hidden dimensions. Biluminosity is Haféz's writing tool, but Haféz is also biluminosity's vehicle of expression.

The following poem clearly depicts the two worlds of biluminosity:

IN NEITHER OCEAN

Go away preacher—What's all this commotion?
It's my heart hurting and you have no notion.

My human balance God crafted from air is
a point so fine it's erased by emotion.

'Til beloved's lips satisfy my desire,
the whole world's advice is babble in motion.

Your servant cannot travel two paths at once;
the prey in your net swims in neither ocean.

Though intoxication has shattered my life,
the seeds of truth arise from that implosion.

O heart, don't groan from beloved's cruelty,
for now you know the sad song of devotion.

Haféz, don't weave tales, don't entice seduction;
I know all the spins and spells of your potion.

In these seven verses, Haféz tells a story set in his unique worldview: a noisy preacher who has no clue, a fragile peace of mind blown away by emotion, obsession with the beloved at the expense of blocking out common sense, the inability to choose between the paths leading to the sacred and profane worlds, a new truth emerging from a shattered dream, a lesson learned from direct experience, and, finally, the biluminous teasing of the poet himself for all his "spins and spells" of levels and meanings. The shattered nature of life from the implosion of intoxication is an oft-repeated theme. This shattering is the disintegration that occurs when we embody the brightness of the divine. Because it is over-whelming compared with our limited experiences, the shattering in turn magnifies the desire for more sustained direct experiences of divine unity. That desire becomes the mystic's lifelong quest.

Part of the genius of Haféz is that he makes use of this same worldview over and over again to tell his tales of tavern and wine and intoxication in verses constantly fresh and eminently insight-ful. The key to the poet's success in presenting this consistent worldview as a backdrop to stories of humanity's search for mean-ing amid a world of unfulfilling choices is that he draws on a vast repertoire of universal reference points to stir his audience's re-sponses. The stories of Jamshid's Cup and its biluminous power of enlightenment flow from the rich diversity of Persian culture. Historical figures show up unexpectedly in the middle of poems:

> *Live your lifetime in the world in such a way*
> *that when you die, they won't say that you died.*

> *Boast not of knowledge, for at the time of death*
> *Aristotle and beggar walk side by side.*

Cutting through a cross section of history, Haféz's world includes ancient Persian, Arabic, Indian, and Chinese mythology and astrology; Old Testament figures such as Joseph, David, and Solomon; Alexander the Great; and Plato and his universal thought forms. Brought into the twentieth century, Haféz undoubtedly would feel right at home discussing Jungian archetypes. A brief examination of the literature available in fourteenth-century Shiraz demonstrates how Haféz could look back into Persia's past influences and embellish biluminosity as the resolution of duality. This philosophy had been taking form and flourishing for many centuries.

From a pre–Zarathustran Sumerian epic about the god Enki comes this quote on the evolution of wisdom: "In the first days, in the very first days, when heaven had moved away from earth and earth had separated from heaven, the father set sail; Enki, the god of wisdom, set sail."[10] And from the *Avesta,* the book of Zarathustra's hymns, emerge these words about the eternal mysteries and the role that love plays in their resolution:"The mysteries of Life that builds His plan doth the Creator of the earth reveal; we'll try to solve these mysteries through Love."[11]

The philosopher Plotinus (205–270 C.E.) was the author of the *Enneads,* the most complete metaphysical text to reach the Islamic world from the Greeks. Known in Arabic as Sheikh, or spiritual master, Plotinus wrote at length on the nature of the soul and the intellect, and his influence can be detected in the work of many Persian poets and philosophers.

From earlier Greek literature came the mathematical teachings of Pythagoras and Niomachus and the writings of Empedocles on natural science and cosmology. Also translated into Arabic were the Hermetic materials, which preserved the inner dimension of the spiritual traditions of Egypt and Greece. These writings, dating from the first to fourth centuries C.E. but probably of a far earlier origin, include the *Poimandres,* attributed to Hermes Trismegistus. The seven Hermetic spiritual principles (mentalism, polarity, gender, cause and effect, rhythm, vibration, and correspondence) still are being paraphrased by twentieth-century teachers as keys to understanding everything from business success to romance. If we look closely, these principles also show up in Haféz as elements of biluminosity.

For well over a thousand years before Haféz, Persians welcomed new systems of thought that arrived via the Silk Road. They imported for study the inward-looking philosophies of Buddhism and Hinduism from India and the socially focused principles of Confucianism and Taoism from China. In the same century that Rudaki began the poetic lineage that eventually culminated with Haféz, the Persian philosopher Avicenna (980–1037) based his story "Salm and Absal" on imported tales about the Buddha. Renowned for his treatises on medicine and psychology, Avicenna wrote an encyclopedia that was widely read in the West and also attempted a synthesis of Islam, Plato, and Aristotle. Like the Persian poets who followed, Avicenna was known for his passion for wine. Like Haféz, in particular, he used world culture as the basis for his philosophical perspectives.

With all this literature available to him, Haféz could put his mind to work in many directions and never run out of riches for references. But his writing was always special, not a copy of anyone else's. When he found his own vision in Jam's Cup, it was his alone. Among the special qualities that Haféz imbued into his philosophy was the need for detachment. For example:

This heart that can see the hidden in Jam's Cup,
why would it suffer from a sad passing loss?

And he also stressed the fragility of the world of spirit:

O you drinking with Jam, best keep your heart pure;
cup's mirror is tarnished by the slightest fog.

The biluminosity of Jamshid's Cup has shifted shapes but is alive and well today, accounting for Haféz's long endurance. This is why the *Divan* has persisted as a divination tool in Middle Eastern popular culture.

Tales are told of extraordinary guidance received from the *Divan* by seekers ranging from England's Queen Victoria to the peasants of many lands over the centuries. That the *Divan* works in this manner is somewhat amazing to anyone comparing its origins to the I Ching or other oracle systems, such as tarot or runes, when we realize that Haféz did not organize his poems into this book and he surely never intended his work to be a divination system. That the *Divan* functions so effectively as an oracle, regardless of how each new editor restructures the volume, can be taken as evidence of a dizzying level of attunement and intelligence at play in its poems to this very day. The invisible level of the spins and spells of that intelligence can be identified as another manifestation of biluminosity.

Today, as we seek calmness amid our computers, pools still reflect images so that we see two sides of every essence, and Haféz still offers us two simultaneous worlds of enlightenment—the physical and the spiritual. He speaks of these worlds in the language of the soul looking into itself. One part of his message stresses that it is not enough just to find Jam's Cup but that we must remain alert to sustain our inner vision of the cup if we are to survive and prosper.

I asked Jam: What became of your globe-wise cup?
He said: Awakened people went back to sleep.

It's said that the theme of Jam's party was
grasp the cup quickly, for Jam will not last.

Haféz, if faith sustained eternally,
the great Jam would never have lost his throne.

Unless we keep the cup's vision, Haféz proclaims, we return to our everyday world with no inspiration and no purpose. This continuous focus on one's inner vision produces the quality that at the cusp of the twenty-first century, we refer to as "sustainability." But, in the spirit of biluminosity, the poet also acknowledges that we are human beings, and, like Jam, our material possessions are subject to loss. He advises us to not take it all so seriously and to remember that a return to spirit is our eternal renewal, the very essence of our evolution. In fact, as we face our daily problems and worries, can anyone offer more profound solace or simpler comfort than this smiling suggestion from Haféz?

At the moment Jamshid's throne and worldly glory
become dust in the wind, don't suffer drink wine.

DON'T DESPAIR WALK ON

Joseph to his father in Canaan shall return, don't despair walk on;
and Jacob's hut will brighten with flowers, don't despair walk on.

Aching hearts heal in time, vanished hopes reappear,
the disparate mind will be pacified, don't despair walk on.

As the spring of life grows the newly green meadow,
roses will crown the sweet nightingale's song, don't despair walk on.

If the world does not turn to your whims these few days,
cosmic cycles are preparing to change, don't despair walk on.

If desperation whispers you'll never know God,
it's the talk of hidden games in the veil, don't despair walk on.

O heart, when the vast flood slashes life to its roots,
Captain Noah waits to steer you ashore, don't despair walk on.

If you trek as a pilgrim through sands to Kaabeh
with thorns lodged deep in your soul shouting why, don't despair walk on.

Though oases hide dangers and your destiny's far,
there's no pathway that goes on forever, don't despair walk on.

My trials and enemies face me on their own,
but mystery always backs up my stand, don't despair walk on.

Haféz, weakened by poverty, alone in the dark,
this night is your pathway into the light, don't despair walk on.

Rend: The Warrior of Life

As you pass by my tomb ask for strength;
here is the prayer house of world's rends.

Life's road is long, Haféz knew, and it can be very difficult. With this in mind, he created a role model for humanity's journey: a freethinker, a nonconformist, a libertine of love, someone who cannot be swayed by fantasy, yet is so in touch with the invisible power of the universe that no division exists between Heaven and Earth. Haféz called his role model—and he called himself—*rend*. In the modern terminology of writers on awareness and spirituality, the rend is known as the spiritual warrior, a seeker of knowledge who embarks on a demanding pathway of discipline toward the goal of enlightened awareness.

The Farsi word for the pathway itself is *rendi*. This pathway runs outside traditional institutions and cuts through culturally established limitations. On this road, the seeker becomes ultracreative, adapting the pursuits of everyday life to an existence that takes meaning from insights gained through exalted states of awareness. Rend is the traveler to whom Haféz speaks in "Don't Despair Walk On," and the poet's persistent refrain provides the simple but complete encouragement necessary to guide the rend through life. Beginning with the ancient story of Joseph's being betrayed by his brothers and sold into slavery and his father Jacob's ensuing grief, Haféz details the trials and tribulations that might make up any person's life. He declares that the consistency of not despairing but just walking on will provide the focus for surviving humanity's inner tests.

In the poem, the rend is faced with an aching heart, lost hope, a disparate mind, the feeling that everything's going wrong, the fear of never finding God, being devastated by life's flood, losing one's way in the desert, and on and on. All this seems to culminate in the seventh verse, about the journey to Kaabeh, Mecca's great cubic structure that Moslem pilgrims circumambulate as a symbolic gesture of faith:

> *If you trek as a pilgrim through sands to Kaabeh*
> *with thorns lodged deep in your soul shouting why, don't*
> > *despair walk on.*

If we listen to the second line of this couplet rather than reading it, our minds understand the double message that whether thorns lodge in your soul or your sole, all you need do is just walk on. This is an oral illustration of biluminosity in action in English, telling us to persevere in both worlds. The poet himself receives his own version of encouragement in the final stanza:

> *Haféz, weakened by poverty, alone in the dark,*
> *this night is your pathway into the light, don't despair*
> > *walk on.*

From lines such as these, some scholars have inferred that Haféz did, indeed, live an impoverished material life and that his words served as a personal statement of courage in the face of need as well as an encouragement to others. But whether we see the poet's "poverty" and "night" as references to his worldly circumstances or humanity's spiritual condition, the advice to "walk on" still applies, for either way is still rendi, the pathway of the rend.

Very little about Haféz's personal life, including his supposed poverty, is recorded outside his own poetry. We do know his approximate birth and death dates and that he traveled very little. Beyond this, the Haféz presented by Western writers to contemporary readers is a being created by six centuries of legends. These tales tell of forty-day vision quests, a relationship with a Shiraz spiritual teacher named Mohammad Attar, and meetings with famous historical figures. English language texts have been repeating these stories for years.

Much less has been said, however, of the ascertainable insights into the poet's spiritual development and the presence of many discernible and meaningful reference points throughout his writing. In essence, the story emerges of a man who worked his way through basic, traditional Islam and left it behind because of the fundamentalism of its practitioners; then turned to the more esoteric spirituality of Sufism until the formal practices of this sect also proved limited in scope and imagination; and eventually discovered a pathway of more direct personal perception of the nature of divinity. This is the story of a rend.

Haféz's use of the word *rend* both expands his own literary tradition and provides a connection to the wisdom teachings of ancient Persia. No one before or since Haféz has used rend to describe the persona and character of the individual spiritual seeker. Over time, rend has come to be identified as the name of his entire body of philosophy. The more usual Farsi meaning of rend, however, is a debauchee. The poet's turning the meaning of rend from debauchee into seeker thus fits perfectly into the well-established Persian metaphor of the wine and tavern and also echoes the extraordinary world of human potentiality.

The Western literary scene first ran into the question of the two meanings of the tavern in Persian literature when British scholar Edward Fitzgerald translated Omar Khayyam's *Rubaiyat* in the mid-nineteenth century. Khayyam, writing three centuries earlier than Haféz, made use of the same tavern imagery, and even Fitzgerald admitted that he first pictured Khayyam literally as an alcoholic hedonist writing about a life of wild times on the Persian bar circuit. This was the prevailing interpretation until the early twentieth century, when better informed Middle Eastern writers, such as Sufi leader Indries Shah, confirmed the wine imagery as representing spiritual ecstasy. More recent editions of the work of Khayyam and other Persian poets take this spiritual view exclusively.

Both wine and Haféz's rend are associated with the glory and traditions of ancient Iran. American archeologists reported in 1996 that they had traced the world's oldest evidence of winemaking to a village near Lake Urumiyeh in northwestern Iran more than seven thousand years ago. But Persian mysticism also has observed intoxicants beyond simply wine. As late as 400 to 500 B.C.E., Persian religious ceremonies included the use of a powerful hallucinogenic drink called *soma,* a practice that inspired a widespread mystical cult in India. Similar substances were used throughout the ancient world's mystery schools, where traditional wisdom was sought during journeys to nonordinary realities.

The West is aware of the existence of these schools in cultures such as Egypt and Greece and their connections across the centuries to current organizations, such as the Freemasons. The origins of Persia's mystery schools are obscured in prehistory, but they apparently started between the end of the Sumerian Empire, about 2000 B.C.E., and the time of Zarathustra, now dated at about 1750 B.C.E. It was during this period in Iran that Zarathustra challenged humanity to look beyond the fear-based perception of the invisible world and trust the balanced order of the single source of creation. The first name given to the one God was Ahura—the wise creator, the projector of pure thought, justice, selfless service, excellence, and the eternal existence of spirit.

Those ancient Iranians were taught that every one of these divine qualities dwells within every person. They also were warned that Ahriman, the destructive twin of Ahura's constructive attributes, is equally potent within our minds. Persian mythology is filled with life and death tales of the war between liberating forces and oppressive demons. This duality in the oneness of creation makes us, the human participants, responsible for how we perceive existence and how we act on the world. Through this perspective, the Iranian people learned the delicate dance between pain and joy, poverty and prosperity, weakness and strength, mind and spirit. They trained their psyches to maintain focus through thick and thin and to stretch the limits of creativity for their own freedom and for the benefit of others.

This essential way of seeing and being spun itself tightly in the colorful carpet of Iran's tumultuous history. During dark times, when wars and violence weakened the nation's confidence, the Persian culture's enlightened poets recalled their ancient roots with magical verses, rhythms, and stories. Such artistry lifted people's spirits, awakened their visions, and inspired them to move forth with renewed energy and hope. During times of disorientation and hard choices, the Persian people awakened within themselves and projected onto the world their ancient wisdom. Thus, Persian history intertwined with the entire world's history.

This unity-within-dualism system of thinking, based on the philosophy of one Creator, seems to have grown out of the old pagan religion of Sun *(mehr)* worship that goes back to prehistory. At the time that Zarathustra established the religion now known by the Greek term Zoroastrianism, this philosophy was practiced in the Mazda religious tradition. Today, the terms Zoroastrianism and Mazdaism are used more or less interchangeably.

The spiritual seeker of Mazda was known as the *mogh,* whose goal was to become one of the evolved humans called Pir-e-Moghan —the same being Haféz identifies as the Elder from whom he seeks guidance in his poems. The poet's writing suggests that to evolve into Pir-e-Moghan is the highest goal of the rend, just as it was for the mogh, and that the key to this personal evolution is finding Jam's Cup within oneself. The ancient pathway to this goal was the cultivation of certain attributes and character traits through participation in community life and daily practices similar to the discipline that we now know as yoga. In fact, it has been claimed that the word *yoga* is derived from the Persian word *yeganeh,* which means unity or wholeness. Many of these traditional practices still are carried on by certain sects of today's dervishes, the ascetic spiritual seekers who have renounced the world.

Both written sources and oral traditions of these ancient times are well known to this day, meaning that Hafez would have had access to them as well. In fact, the oldest surviving edition of Zarathustra's book, the *Avesta,* dates back to its reproduction in Hafez's own fourteenth century. Some stories say that the original *Avesta* was written in gold ink on specially prepared ox hides and kept in the city of Estakhr, where it was destroyed by Alexander the Great. Hafez may be referring to this golden writing and its true imperishability in this verse:

Wisdom etched in golden script on pure topaz:
Be generous in life or why be at all?

The Persian mystery academy was called the *mehrab* and provided a monastery-type training for the soul. According to the writings of Mahmoudi Bakhtiari in *Rahi be Maktab-e Hafez (A Path to the School of Hafez),* published in 1966 in Iran, these academies were housed in eastward-facing, dome-shaped structures with the Moon and stars painted on the inside of the domes. Openings on the eastern walls permitted rays of the rising Sun to enter at dawn, suggesting all-night meditations and rituals.

The intent of these schools was to create a replication of life on Earth within the dome in order to train initiates to realize their life's purpose as work, which was defined as service to the divine attributes of humanity. The foundation of the school was education and training built around a curriculum emphasizing the keeping of secrets, loyalty and faithfulness, kindness, and disciplined, vigorous work. The essential qualities developed by successful initiates in the mehrab were the same that Hafez attributes to the rend: joy, pleasure, and love.

Although the domes of the past, painted with the Moon and stars, had long vanished by Hafez's time, the poet apparently found Shiraz's taverns a perfect location for extending these ancient concepts. With the Islamic-controlled establishment opposed to the use of alcohol, the taverns were owned by the minority Christians and Zoroastrians. It was here that Shiraz's rends met to converse and create a culture unique to the taverns themselves. This culture even included designated "elders" who ordered drinks. As the mogh of old sought in sacred domes to become Pir-e-Moghan, so did Haféz's rends seek in their spiritual taverns for the elusive biluminosity of the spirit contained in Jam's Cup:

I search for God whether in mosque or tavern;
God is my desire and there is nothing else.

At times, the taverns were closed down by the city officials. Some of Haféz's best-known lines are concerned with these episodes:

They have closed the tavern doors—O God, do not condone,
for they open the doors of lies and hypocrisy.

And the reopening as well:

Thank God the tavern door opens today
and I can enter when I feel the need.

One can imagine the scene in old Shiraz's taverns, with Haféz and his fellow rends, whether Elders of spirit or friends of the wine cup of philosophy, sitting about and articulating ancient teachings in then-modern terminology. The process might bear a striking resemblance to the late twentieth century's spiritual movement, which has involved the recovery and restatement of many relevant ancient teachings and traditions.

From the basic principles derived from the mehrab—joy, pleasure, and love—spring a series of other qualities attributed by Haféz to his own version of warrior and pathway. These attributes of the rend can be summarized as follows:

The rend is dissatisfied with limitations and strives to go beyond them. The reason is twofold: to stretch the imagination and to get to the truth of matters. In this way, the rend embodies the spirit and science of inquiry and continuously questions the established order. But the rend also lives in ways consistent with alternative thinking. To the rend, philosophy and everyday life are inseparable. The process and the goal are one and the same. This is the path of directness.

Whatever comes to seeker adds to her fortune;
on the direct path, O heart, no one goes astray.

The rend is the antithesis of *zahed*—a person whose puritanism is circumscribed by the laws of a particular viewpoint and set of practices. Zahed, like rend, is a word with opposing meanings. As rend is turned from debauchee to evolved human in Haféz's work, zahed is a pure person turned to hypocritical puritan. Contrary to the zahed, who does not think freely but is instead the follower of strict ideas, the rend is a freespirited libertine who absorbs life through direct perception every moment. Fundamentalism— stringent attachment and rigidity of thought and action—is anti-rend in Hafez's poetry, and he aims many a criticism at Shiraz's zaheds.

A wine seller who is free of hypocrisy
is preferred to deceptive vendor of piety.

The rend is openhearted, receptive to new ideas, and enthusiastically absorptive of every iota of phenomena. This is the state of unity at odds with the remoteness and hypocrisy of the zahed. In unity, the rend is aware that the hidden treasure of knowledge is like a pearl in the seashell. On the one hand, you get to the pearl through careful and painstaking work. On the other hand, the seashell itself is subject to cumulative expansion: the residues of the previous stages of growth remain clearly part of the structure and design of the subsequent stages. As such, the rend feels in full continuity with the rest of creation—past, present, and future.

Cherish the way of rendi, for this secret path,
like the journey to treasure, is not known to all.

The rend is in love with life. She sees and seeks beauty and pleasure and delights in imagination and the process of rejoicing. The rend is intoxicated and, in the eyes of the world's zaheds, sinful. But danger from a "bad reputation" does not concern the rend, for she is aware of the zahed's hypocrisy and unfortunate inability to enjoy life to the fullest. To the rend, the zahed's falsehood and words of condemnation are not deterrents. Instead, they offer a mirror of remindfulness about how grand life's potential is and how one should ride the waves of this massive potential every instant.

I stroll the bazaar, search all of Shiraz,
in quest of a single pure joyous soul.

But only the rends, those libertine-loves,
pursue the freedom of joy as their goal.

The rend is revolutionary in spirit and evolutionary in thought. He knows that quantum leaps are necessary to break mental and social barriers and light up a new star in the sky of imagination. At the same time, however, the rend is timely in his assessments and actions. Rebellion does not take place for its own sake but rather for the purpose of bringing about deep transformation at a time when it can have the most impact. Because of this innate timeliness, the rend is patient, fearless of pain and harsh conditions, and still joyful and in a relaxed state of mind during periods of turbulence or public apathy. Faithful to the belief in the power of the mystery of the universe, the rend is centered, does not complain, and is free of expectations.

Road of riches is walked without wounded heart;
insistence and force do not yield Paradise.

The rend is the compassionate, empathetic embracer of the world's pain. Unseparated from the Creator, unafraid to embrace existence as it is, the rend takes on and deals with the darkness as well as the light. But in fully embracing the world, the rend also remains completely detached. This detachment fully embodies compassion and also serves as a tool for unprejudiced engagement in constructive actions.

> *Sometimes I am Haféz, other times a dreg-drinker;*
> *see this freedom I find within creative power.*

The rend is a freespirited and humanistic warrior, willing to risk everything at every moment in the battle against hypocrisy and falsehood, the creators of discord and separation. But the rend is also sharp in skills. She is talented and continuously upgrades her talents in order to penetrate further the ultimate nature of reality. The rend's skills include artistic imagination, sober intoxication, specific techniques, the ability to ask illuminating questions, and the capacity to walk the razor's edge through all paradoxes. The first and final vision of the rend is one thing only: truth.

This means that true creativity is concerned with clear and accurate vision, not with fantasy, not with pinning labels on the unknown.

> *O purist zahed, rends' ways don't bemoan;*
> *you won't have to pay for sins not your own.*

> *If I'm good or bad, just tend your own crop;*
> *one harvests only that which one has sown.*

> *Please don't moralize about judgment day;*
> *why label "good" or "bad" the veiled unknown?*

> *Haféz, don't compromise secret of life*
> *that Creator's pen wrote on only your stone.*

The training process of the mehrab also was designed to do away with three elements common to unenlightened humanity: tendencies toward complaint and cries of neediness; the practices of hypocrisy and lying; and the inflicting of pain, grief, and harm on body or soul. These conditions were seen as "enemies of life" by the ancients, and they also emerge as the principal qualities of the self-righteous hypocritical zaheds, the enemies of Haféz's rends.

As we refocus these wisdom teachings from the past into the present, we find ourselves facing the task of becoming a particular kind of human being at this point in humanity's evolutionary spiral. The type of being we're becoming is one who will not only survive but can also prosper and endure in the face of the demands of the upcoming century and the present Information Age. The rend is an ideal archetype for this future and one that is not foreign to our contemporary consciousness.

The spirit that Haféz attributes to the rend is the rebellious spirit of individualism that has long characterized the Western world in general and America in particular. It is the spirit of the person who combines a distinct, nontraditional personal path of success with an element of spiritual awareness and some form of artistic expression. It is easy to make up subjective lists of rend spirits who have inspired our culture. Such European poets as William Blake, Rimbaud, Baudelaire, and Goethe embodied forms of this rend energy, as did Emily Dickinson, Ralph Waldo Emerson, Henry David Thoreau, and Walt Whitman in America. The twentieth century has seen several rend incarnations: Ernest Hemingway and Gertrude Stein of the Lost Generation in 1920's Paris; folksinger Woody Guthrie during the Great Depression years; the Beat Generation's Jack Kerouac and Allen Ginsburg; and in recent years, poet-singers Leonard Cohen, Joan Baez, and Bob Dylan; actor James Dean; poet Maya Angelou, and novelist Isabelle Allende. As even this short list demonstrates, the essence of the rend is easily identifiable in current Western culture. The list could go on and on, but our purpose is not to argue who would fit into Haféz's model of the rend and who would not.

As Haféz is quick to point out, paradox always exists. If we attempt to take these personal images of the rend as role models, we are taking a step away from rendi. One's true path is one's own unique path. Rends may recognize one another, but it's not because they are similar. Rather, it's because they recognize the heart of rendi in one another. It is a mistake to associate being a rend with any particular way of talking, behaving, or comporting oneself. Traveling rendi demands the perception of unity in diversity and also diversity in unity. From the day of our creation, Haféz proclaims, all this is in our own hands.

How then, the question arises, does one become a rend? Where is the pathway called rendi? In the verse that opened this chapter, the poet offers a suggestion that has been observed by Iranians for centuries and that goes out to the rest of the world as well:

As you pass by my tomb ask for strength;
here is the prayer house of world's rends.

Just as the mehrab was the prayer house of the ancient mogh, and just as the taverns of Shiraz were Haféz's classrooms of life, the poet identifies his own tomb as the prayer house for the present and future rends of the world. His tomb, in this reference, can be seen as much more than just the spot where he happens to be buried. We can envision the tomb as the body of work through which he remains known in this life. His poetry, therefore, is Haféz's legacy of personal alchemy through which the spiritual seeker learns to travel rendi. In the verse, as well as in the advice of "Don't Despair Walk On," Haféz establishes the theme that has carried his message through the ages: If we wish to survive and prosper, the pathway called rendi offers a marvelous opportunity of biluminous enlightenment as the guiding light for our endurance.

Part 2 of this book, which guides us from the tavern of the human spirit into a place of study we call the school of alchemy, presents a series of concepts that are both the tools and attributes of rendi. As with so much of Haféz's wisdom, these principles have emerged from a primordial time, yet they remain as relevant today and to the future as they have proved to be during centuries past. This pathway offers humanity access to a chalice of unlimited potential that has been sustained by our global history. We now have the opportunity to do our part in the evolution of that potential.

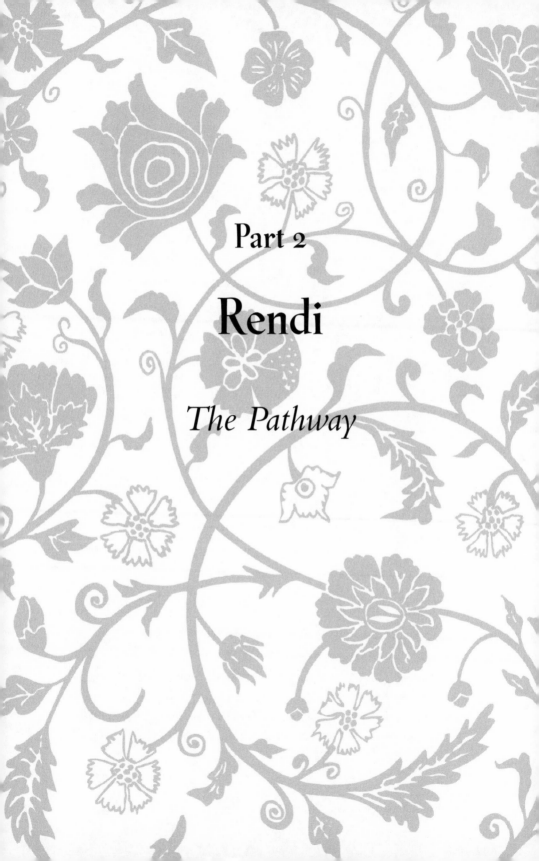

Part 2

Rendi

The Pathway

To Study the Poet

*H*aféz created a body of poetry that has inspired awe and wonder among distant admirers as well as admiration and study in his homeland. But to study the poet's philosophy in depth has been difficult for non-Farsi speakers simply because not enough of his verse has been translated within an informed context. In addition, virtually every line of every poem has been interpreted to offer multiple meanings even in the original language.

Lacking a clearly defined linear process for assessing the teachings that emerge from the poems, those who would study Haféz are forced into a more heartfelt analysis of his offerings. The student must love the poet enough to delve into his writings while extending patience and understanding to the point of extracting and embracing his wisdom.

Aspiring to write this book, we as co-authors started with just that type of love and approach. We discovered, however, that we needed to develop another quality if we wanted to present the philosophy of Haféz in an intelligible, accessible form. We needed imaginative organization—a way of putting together the basic fundamentals of the poet's thinking without turning his teachings into that which he hated most: fundamentalism itself.

The first principle of our approach became the explanation of basic messages of individual poems. The second part of the organization involved a step-by-step plotting of his many ideas, taking into consideration the influences of the environment in which the poet lived. This plotting became our understanding of the pathway called rendi. Through the study of his poetry, these steps emerge as a road that we, as readers and listeners, may walk.

To structure this pathway, we have needed the help of generations of Iranian scholars who have organized and categorized the thousands of Haféz couplets and then drawn from them a systematic way of thinking. Our synthesis of the pathway of the rend takes its roots from the work of a number of these scholars. Although the twenty steps are offered here in a seemingly chronological order, they need not be seen exclusively in this manner. Each step is a starting point, a goal, and a full process within itself.

For validation of these concepts, however, we have looked beyond the scholars and into the everyday lives of contemporary Iranians who sense in the poet a kindred spirit who feels their pain, awakens their desire for joy and freedom, and supports them through their moments of fear and self-doubt. Haféz, quite simply, is the most popular poet in this culture. He is quoted and paraphrased continually as people go about their daily activities. His wisdom may be the basis of discussions on trade, politics, philosophy, or the beauty of a Persian rug. His deep compassion is felt, six hundred years after his passing, as readers sense Haféz speaking with them individually. He speaks about the shadow—the deepest secret and fear of every person, an element close to the surface for many Iranians, with their extreme historical swings of independence and slavery—and he thereby becomes accessible to every reader.

Communicating the basis of this passion of virtually an entire culture for the beloved mystical poet thus became the goal of our articulation of the pathway known as rendi. What has evolved is a twenty-step statement of the perennial philosophy, reshaped and related as only the pen of Haféz could do it. Therefore, although the poet did not put these teachings together in an anthology or training manual, we believe they are accurate reflections of the mystical lessons he drew from his own alchemical classroom and applied to his artistry in order to offer us all a vision into humanity's potential.

As in the poet's own verses, the pages ahead will present the essence of the wisdom of Haféz in various contexts and with many different reference points. Within the conceptual frame-work of an alchemical school, we apply the pedagogical approach of reinforcing through repetition the points made in each chapter. This method intends to preserve the essential quality of Haféz's poetry—the interconnectedness of individual parts. It is through awareness of this web of relationships that we, as readers, can participate actively in the poetry. We grasp each particle (word) and form a thread (step). Then, by weaving these threads together, a unified carpet of the whole appears.

THE SCHOOL OF ALCHEMY

O youth with no knowledge of ancient ways bold,
before you can tell, you must hear what you're told.

O child now enrolled in the classroom of truth,
hear from the Elder what you'll learn when you're old.

As seeker you must leave the gross world behind
so philosopher's stone can melt you to gold.

Your listening is dulled by food and by sleep;
dissolve these false needs and return to the mold.

When love's hottest rays penetrate heart and soul,
you'll burn so with God even sunshine feels cold.

Drown yourself without fear in God's deepest sea;
your curls won't be dampened when legends unfold.

Surrender comforts, give your sight to the blind;
the bright light of God your new self will uphold.

If sincerely you seek God as companion,
no doubt can exist you will bond in the fold.

Embrace life's foundation, its highs and its lows;
empty your heart 'til every craving is sold.

O Haféz, if unity indeed is your dream,
be as dust on the floor where school's carpet unrolled.

Step 1

Ancient Ways

*T*he first step for any mystic seeker is to find an appropriate pathway into higher awareness. Rendi was both Haféz's choice and his creation. On this pathway, the material and spiritual worlds come into balance. Its concepts grow out of the distant past and await only our current awakening in order to flourish anew. If you are interested in following Haféz's lead, his verses will guide you.

Rendi begins with a visit to the school of alchemy, where personal growth is sought and taught. For Haféz, this school is the tavern where he drinks wine. It is also the domed mehrab of the ancient mogh, the composing studio of the musician, the church of the Christian, the vision quest site of native peoples worldwide, the private room of the modern meditator, and the visionary space of virtual reality travelers wearing glasses and gloves. The school is whatever pathway we choose. For you, the reader, this book is offered as one classroom.

Throughout the Middle Ages and for hundreds of years thereafter, scholars and scientists spent many futile, frustrating hours, days, and lifetimes attempting to convert base metals into gold through alchemical formulas. From early mythologies they had

heard tales of alchemy, a secret process that could transform ordi-
nary essence into a substance of great value. Their quest, Haféz
pointed out, was a prime example of confusing the two worlds of
existence. The powerful alchemy of mythology involves the trans-
formation of the inner, invisible world of humanity. And while
modern chemistry is not that far from realizing the basic ideas of
the metallurgical alchemists, the need for personal growth still
dominates the consciousness of every human.

If we see the purpose of rendi as spiritual enlightenment, the
function of the school of alchemy becomes the step-by-step pro-
cess of learning how to recognize the essence and relevance of the
dawning of this new awareness. Exposure to alternative realities
without understanding their true nature certainly is possible—it
can happen, for instance, during unguided, drug-induced experi-
ences. But in order to fulfill our inner potential and to participate
as both student and channel of the universal mystic process, the
school experience is a great help.

"The School of Alchemy" is also the title we have given to
the poem at the start of this chapter. In this composition, the
poet's most clearly stated guidance for personal questing, Haféz
welcomes the seeker to the search:

> O youth with no knowledge of ancient ways bold,
> before you can tell, you must hear what you're told.

> O child now enrolled in the classroom of truth,
> hear from the Elder what you'll learn when you're old.

Haféz, so far as we know, created no schools during his life-
time. He established no identifiable teaching system. Yet the path-
way he pictures and the process he details in "The School of
Alchemy" leave no doubt that here was a master of universal mys-
tic tradition as well as of poetry. He speaks of spiritual practices
common to vision-seeking the world around:

> As seeker you must leave the gross world behind
> so philosopher's stone can melt you to gold.

Your listening is dulled by food and by sleep;
dissolve these false needs and return to the mold.

Legends tell us that the poet did indeed fast and maintain long vigils in search of answers to his own desire to master reality. He explains commitment and trust in the competence of the mystery that guides the search process:

Drown yourself without fear in God's deepest sea;
your curls won't be dampened when legends unfold.

Surrender comforts, give your sight to the blind;
the bright light of God your new self will uphold.

Embrace life's foundation, its highs and its lows;
empty your heart 'til every craving is sold.

The pathway yields rewards:

When love's hottest rays penetrate heart and soul,
you'll burn so with God even sunshine feels cold.

And it imparts the comfort resulting from transcendence:

If sincerely you seek God as companion,
no doubt can exist you will bond in the fold.

The poem's final couplet gives the secret to the seeker: Be humble, be open, soak up the wisdom of personal alchemy like a spiritual sponge:

O Haféz, if unity indeed is your dream,
be as dust on the floor where school's carpet unrolled.

The process offers itself to every person. Simply being alive is to be enrolled in the school of alchemy. For Haféz, the study of personal evolution is a completely natural and inevitable feature of existence, as evidenced in the following lines from another poem (the phrase "first day" indicates the moment of creation):

On first day when we breathed in love and rendi,
we agreed then to entrust no other way.

But while the invitation goes out to all, never doubt that the school itself is a unique and special place:

> *Rise and come with me, a traveler, to the tavern;*
> *you'll see in that circle what a special place I have.*

As we travel rendi together in the coming chapters, we will be guided through various signposts and ideas that are at the heart of the personal philosophy of Haféz. Keep in mind that the last thing the poet advocates is to be a fundamentalist zahed preaching any particular doctrine. Haféz was a man who excelled in and loved the Koran, who was intimately familiar with the religious practices of his time, and who chose the most expansive, enlivening pathway he could find. Therefore, although his verses speak of fasting, for instance, it is doubtful that he would hold up any one practice as being the only passageway into awareness. What he is stressing is focused personal discipline in whatever way you choose. Every pathway has its own demands, and those demands will be just as intense as extended fasting and vigilance.

As you enter the school of alchemy, Haféz cautions, be aware of what is being presented to you each step of the way. In short—and in twentieth-century terminology—don't get caught up in a cult. Gain a clear picture of rendi as you begin your walk; then keep your heart open and your mind sharp as you proceed. Seek the company of true friends who wish only to share your wine cup, not those who would construct a hierarchy of leaders and followers. This is the test of a school of truth:

> *Haféz, don't follow strangers with blind obedience;*
> *instead, make your friends among the devoted rends.*

As previously pointed out, Haféz's verses testify that he journeyed through organized religions before finding his own path. He comments often about taking off or pawning his woolen cloak—the term *Sufi* is said to derive from an Arabic word signifying ascetics who wore coarse woolen garments. Like so many other searchers, including many in our contemporary culture,

Haféz next turned to ancient teachings. He states his feelings clearly in the following verse about Khaneghah, a Sufi monastery:

> *Don't expect lovemaking secrets at Khaneghah;*
> *wine of moghan you can drink only with moghan.*

And these lines he addresses to the sheikh, or traditional religious teacher:

> *I am devotee of Elder, O sheikh,*
> *for he delivered that which you promised.*

Here, once again, the term for Elder is Pir-e-Moghan, the timeless evolved being and the aspiring rend's role model. Traveling on the caravan of existence and seeing the triumphs and regressions of humanity since its inception, the Elder evokes in Haféz an exquisite mélange of the best in post-Mazda's divine unity and prehistory's pagan traditions: oneness with nature, celebration of life, authentic joy, embrace of the feminine, egalitarianism, focused discipline, and compassionate action. These also are the qualities you will find stressed in your personal school of alchemy, whatever it may be.

Giving Way to the Flow

In prayer I recalled your eyebrows' curved wake;
the feeling it brought made the prayer house quake.

Do not expect of me patient and sober;
that endurance I lost I can't ever fake.

The cup's purely empty, the birds are all drunk;
for only love and good work can we time take.

I hear much talk of progress in world affairs;
flowers offer rapture, West Wind spreads joy's flake.

O bride of art, don't complain of creation;
here is your groom, make an altar for his sake.

The devas of trees are all wearing jewels,
but beloved's beauty does nature full make.

Trees huddled together share each other's weight,
but cypress, free from grief, soars far from this stake.

Musician, play well for these words of Haféz;
these happy memories bring tears of sweet ache.

Step 2

Making the Prayer House Quake

You are a seeker. You are traveling the pathway called rendi, walking in the footsteps of Haféz. Furthermore, as you begin rendi, you have committed to a course of study in the school of alchemy. But what, you wonder, is the nature of the journey that lies ahead? Whatever adventures await, their essence must address the central question of all seekers: How do we bring the elements of higher awareness into our everyday life in order to discover and nurture the sacred in the banal? We sense that successfully facilitating the evolution of the soul through practical living makes life on Earth fulfilling and allows the mature soul to achieve its intended dimension.

In the poem "Giving Way to the Flow," Haféz suggests that one such adventure can occur during the simple and direct act of prayer. Many spiritual philosophies report that some sort of metaphysical jolt is necessary to shake the human being out of the self-satisfied state of mind that denies the inner desire to pursue the unbounded, invisible world of spirit. This jolt sometimes is perceived as "the call" to be a minister or servant of a particular religious or spiritual order. For other people, it is simply an awakening. For Haféz, the image of the beloved's eyebrows rattles the very prayer house:

In prayer I recalled your eyebrows' curved wake;
the feeling it brought made the prayer house quake.

Awakened by the experience, the poet realizes he can never go
back to what he was. His world is changed. He sees even the birds
as intoxicated beings, and he devotes himself to just two pursuits:

Do not expect of me patient and sober;
that endurance I lost I can't ever fake.

The cup's purely empty, the birds are all drunk;
for only love and good work can we time take.

The poem goes on to celebrate the new perceptions of this
state of being: rapture, joy, creativity, beauty, and freedom. The
final verse captures the mood and music of the experience:

Musician, play well for these words of Haféz;
these happy memories bring tears of sweet ache.

The quaking of the prayer house and the deep feeling that
follows represent but one step along the path of rendi. As you
continue to travel, however, there are common characteristics
that your own trip will share with the journey of Haféz. The
school of alchemy offers eight guidelines, drawn from the poet's
own verses, for dealing with the tests of rendi. Here are the eight:

You are surrounded by one thousand and one fantasies. Be aware.
Do not pause for unnecessary disputes and futile arguments that
obscure your opportunity for direct perception of reality. Instead,
let your closed heart open.

O heart, like closed flower bud, don't complain;
dawn wind brings the breeze to open your knot.

Trust that "competent mystery" guides your affairs. Do not lose
heart when life becomes difficult. Trust makes you cheerful and
lighthearted.

Do not grieve over the profane world, drink wine;
agitation is a waste for a wise heart.

Be vigilant—paradox is everywhere. Don't become caught up in thinking that there's only one way to be. Dancing with paradox demands agility and humor.

In the end, my home will be the valley of silence;
for now, I raise an uproar to the dome of Heaven.

Addiction to grief haunts you in the form of the archetype of the abandoned child. Welcome the opportunity to release this archetype. Accept, with a smile, responsibility for all aspects of your existence.

Don't complain of suffering on the path of knowledge;
she who has not labored is not prepared to arrive.

Embrace everything. Release fear. Give of yourself. This is love. Express love through your art, whatever its form, and unify yourself with your object of creation, with all creation.

I am lover and rend and admirer of beauty;
let your own eyes see these many talents I possess.

This unity of creator and created is the essence of service. Through service, you embody the eternal flow of generosity. Give to life as the Sun gives light to you.

In her service, particle-like, whirling,
I fly to the source of luminous Sun.

This flow of generosity dissolves self-centeredness, harmfulness, malice, and jealousy. Desire for attention vanishes into humility, making surrender easier. You become more creative, move forward, stretch, increase dynamism, and ignite the fire of passion.

> *God gave you beauty in destiny's bridal room;*
> *what need can you have for an earthly beautician?*

One task consumes you: seeking and expressing truth.

> *Kind cupbearer, may your chalice always be full,*
> *and may wisdom heal all this pain of hangover.*

You will find these eight concepts explained, repeating, expanding, and interweaving all along your rendi journey. As you sit alone in whatever form your personal prayer may take, the arrival of spirit into your life may be heralded by a quaking prayer house or by a silent, profound feeling. But however spirit arrives, it will be summoning you to see and understand a powerful new aspect of yourself, an aspect that will respond to these eight guidelines. For Haféz, that awakening aspect of himself became what he called the "gathered memory."

Our Life on Earth

She who walks with gathered mind and a loving friend
happily and with destiny her way will wend.

Gateway to love's sanctuary surpasses reason;
who kisses that threshold offers life to the rend.

Her rosebud mouth is the red ring of Solomon
where the whole world's image is the light she will lend.

Ruby lips and black hair are like charms we can't name;
let me hold beloved whose beauty I commend.

So long as on Earth you live, do value your strength;
the wheel of life buries all weakness in the end.

O mighty one, don't look down on the weak and lean;
the pauper on love's path to the heights will ascend.

The prayer of the poor averts misery from life;
what yield from a crop when you the farmer offend?

My secret of love West Wind tells to beauty king,
that same king to whom Jam and Kay Khosrow knees bend.

And if king rejects a poor lover like Haféz,
assure him a sultan to a pauper may tend.

Step 3

Gathered Memory

*I*n the school of alchemy, where the prayer house sometimes quakes, each student follows a unique course of study. Every step and every test are designed for that person alone. Still, there is one curriculum common to all of humanity, past and present. The featured teaching in that curriculum is the concept of the gathered memory. This is a literal translation of Haféz's term *khater-e majmou*.

This gathered memory is a condition of unity created by weaving disparate thoughts, emotions, and personalities into one sharply focused image. It emerges both from within and without, arising in each person as the world of both one's self and one's double—that ancient metaphysical shadow being that is said to be an image of the self as it appears in the spirit world.

You sometimes may experience gathered memory as completely relaxed composure. It is a peaceful state obtained through a momentary, yet complete flash of aggregate memory. You know who you are, where you've come from, and who and what you are related to. This is not a matter of family or ancestry but, more expansively, a fact of interconnectedness with the rest of creation—past, present, and future. This realization, if arrived at

with authenticity and depth of perception, can evoke instantly a
deep feeling of support and a nurturing environment for perse-
verance and visionary forward motion.

The wholism of the gathered memory has its roots in the
imagery of the beloved's disheveled hair, the symbol of life's wind-
ing roads and weaving ups and downs. This bright black hair is
intrinsically loving and protective because it casts a temporarily
inconvenient but ultimately liberating shadow over a sunlike face
that peers at you through fiery eyes and allows you to lose your
self-centeredness in its majestic beauty.

The opening couplet of "Our Life on Earth," the poem at the
start of this chapter, illustrates how Haféz uses khater-e majmou:

> She who walks with gathered mind and a loving friend
> happily and with destiny her way will wend.

As the beloved with her gathered memory becomes the entry
point into higher awareness, the dominance of reason in one's life
lessens and the warriorship of the rend arises:

> Gateway to love's sanctuary surpasses reason;
> who kisses that threshold offers life to the rend.

In the next verse, Haféz gives us one of his most significant
and ancient images: the red ring of Solomon. He declares that the
beloved's mouth is like that ring through which our enlightened
universe appears:

> Her rosebud mouth is the red ring of Solomon
> where the whole world's image is the light she will lend.

In the mythology of the Middle East, King Solomon's ring
carries a very special significance. Renowned for his wisdom in
matters of justice and for the wealth of his realm, Solomon also is
said to have communed with animals. This special gift was his
secret of guidance, and the tool that gave him this gift was his
magical ring. Thus, in the shamanistic tradition common to vir-
tually every ancient culture on Earth—and a tradition that has

been revived in late-twentieth-century spirituality—animals' voices are acknowledged as a pathway to knowledge. Haféz draws on this idea many times, including in his classic poem "The Wild Deer," which is featured in part 4 of this book. It is significant that in "Our Life on Earth" such guidance is aligned with the gathered memory.

The succeeding verses deliver a message of compassion for the weak and lean and poor. This is the poet's "secret of love" that the West Wind, that messenger of ancient traditions, shares with beauty king, a ruler so powerful as to be honored by the great Jam and his descendant, Kay Khosrow. In the final verse, the balance of all life and the sanctity of all beings is emphasized:

> *And if king rejects a poor lover like Haféz,*
> *assure him a sultan to a pauper may tend.*

In addition to spiritual guidance and the secret of compassion, other attributes of gathered memory appear throughout the poetry. Here is a summary of this condition of mind that can be attained by study in the school of alchemy:

Gathered memory is a timeless, personal mission, a divine intent on Earth. All answers are within the rend, not outside. One's focus must be inward to see personal divinity. No amount of grieving about the outside world will result in clarity of vision. One must release the yearning, passion, and intent from within.

> *Don't get down on your knees in futile mourning;*
> *daily bread does not grow or shrink with your grief.*

> *Because these futile cries bring no benefits,*
> *be farsighted or sorrow becomes heart's thief.*

Gathered memory activates an intelligence so fierce that it is fearless of limitations that stop others. This fierceness is devoid of guilt, repentance, and pity. Rendi thus becomes its own weapon of war against hypocrisy and against falsehood.

Lovemaking and the cup must remain my core;
I've repented one hundred times—but no more.

Gathered memory is a pathway of inner nobility, a clear sincerity free from the calculation of profit and loss. Inherent in this road is unconditional faith in the competence of the universe and the confidence of the individual to fully align with the eternal flow of life for the optimum benefit of all elements of creation.

Purely by chance, the name of Haféz is honored;
for the true rend, there is neither profit nor loss.

Gathered memory projects global thinking from a sacred point of view. Immersion in rendi results in a deep belief in democracy, peacemaking, and expansiveness, as well as a deep opposition to the convenient compromise that dilutes truth.

Haféz, rends need not worry about unity of heart;
at creation, God freed us of need for duplicity.

Gathered memory is about excellence, lofty effort, and achieving our utmost capacity, even if it is accomplished through restraint and silence. It takes time and patience to develop true inner strength.

Do not count on reaching the place of great beings
until you gather up the tools of great beings.

Gathered memory is the field of surrender for abandonment of the world's pain and pleasure. Ordinary, everyday affairs become fields of sacred practice and spiritual transformation. The mind and heart are freed from ego concerns to move on to deeper activities. True freedom results only when you abandon your worries about the outer world and commit to trusting the competent mystery of creation.

Haféz, if you leave your affairs to God's wisdom,
you can have a lot of fun with your destiny.

Gathered memory leads to the realization that service to life and to other people is the natural result of the perception of humanity's connectedness to all life. In this context, service is not something to think about doing; it's simply a natural activity as higher awareness dawns and moves the rend to the cusp of creativity.

If wind brings to me a scent from your street,
in joy I bestow globe's soul to the wind.

As we walk rendi in order to assemble our personal gathered memories, we must be aware of the world around us, its agendas, and our own reactions and responses to those agendas. That is our next subject in the school of alchemy.

My Business Deal with Mystery

Who sings to the kings my pauper's serenade?
We rends two thousand Jams for one cup will trade.

If this wine's unseasoned and that other's aged,
our fresh one a thousand times better is made.

Old man, don't distract me with beads for prayers;
I'm not one of those birds on whom you have preyed.

Though laws I've broken and reputation ruined,
my friends again will lift my name from the shade.

You, elixir merchant, examine my heart;
while I have no funds, all my love is well paid.

Where shall I grieve? Who will hear my sad story?
Your lips fed my breath but away you did fade.

My disloyal beloved speaks not to me;
no message by pen, no hello am I bade.

Your kindness could buy my service forever;
I'm a sweet-tempered servant free from tirade.

Though lashes flash arrows to spill Haféz's blood,
no such killer of revenge need be afraid.

Step 4

The Goal of Truth

*T*he traveling rend must be fully focused on the goal of truth. But focus is difficult because we live in a world of humanity that is filled with a multiplicity of agendas. Diffusion, lies, and double standards are everywhere. Everyone tries to sell you something, to convince you that your power resides in what they have. Every cluster of personalities sings a different chant. Each tries to lure you into thinking that you are one of them. But a rend is a free spirit and does not ache to be like others because it is safer to follow than to create anew. A rend thinks independently and chooses a finely tuned pathway. Haféz says to the rend: Be careful but bold, use your intelligence, and let the wine of truth and love run through every cell of your body and keep you soberly intoxicated.

In "My Business Deal with Mystery," the rend is willing to remain a singing pauper, to trade two thousand Jams—those great kings of the material world—for one cup of wine:

Who sings to the kings my pauper's serenade?
We rends two thousand Jams for one cup will trade.

The preference for new wine (or wisdom or bliss) over old, after

all, is a matter of taste. And if the new is all that we have, then
we're happy with that:

> *If this wine's unseasoned and that other's aged,*
> *our fresh one a thousand times better is made.*

The goal of truth, says the poet, is not a matter of formal
prayers. Furthermore, those who sell religion are merely preying
on the gullible. Rather than relying on the prayer beads of others,
the rend makes his own deal with mystery in order to pursue the
goal of truth:

> *Old man, don't distract me with beads for prayers;*
> *I'm not one of those birds on whom you have preyed.*

The reward for choosing one's own path is the enhanced in-
tegrity of one's gathered memory. You are able to stand on your
own feet, mentally and spiritually. This integrity manifests as each
individual rend's intent and will. As the rend surrenders to the
pathway, the focus on truth becomes undivided, pure, complete,
and irreversible. Consider this verse:

> *Whatever effort I've made has been all in search,*
> *all to keep destiny upright on my pathway.*

Although the goal of truth is unity, the pathway itself always
requires fragmentation. This curious paradox is laughable, Haféz
says, but we must accept it. To become whole we must first allow
ourselves to shatter:

> *I aspired to mastery but became your slave;*
> *I desired sultanhood but chose service instead.*

The mere image of the beloved has this very effect on Haféz:

> *These two eyes don't sleep because of thoughts of you;*
> *this heart will never rest while apart from you.*

But it is precisely the pain of separation, the breaking of the
heart, that ignites and reinforces the fire of the rend's desire for
truth. The union, the truth, is with the larger force of creation,

but it is one that is not to be searched for on the outside. The seeds of unity are found and sown within one's own being. There is a clear and unique pathway for everyone. Each person must search for it and find it. A singular source binds us all, yet we each have our own distinct way to get to it. This is the paradox of unity: a multiplicity of pathways within the vision of a single force.

The tale of love is only one story but it's wondrous,
for every new version I hear is unique in itself.

Love is the point of intersection between one's intended path and the balanced functioning of the larger environment. Love is also the energy that flows both through the intersection as well as through the expanded space of our existence. This realization is one manifestation of truth. The poet's mystical perspective sees life as the process of embracing all truth to the point of sensing it so fully that you become one with it. This oneness is the essence of compassion. You feel someone else's pain, you share in the world's joy, or you understand someone else's dream as if it were your own.

To be something, you must have the desire to become. This is the female principle of creation. The yearning in the object to be created releases the energy necessary for that yearning to transform into intent and will. Intent, in turn, finds the tools necessary for the yearning to materialize. The coming together of the yearning and the tools is what we often refer to as synchronicity. It is when our desire for something coincides with the universe's desire for the same thing. When the two come together, manifestation occurs. Sometimes when we observe such a phenomenon, we simply call it magic. For the poet, it is merely one more form of truth.

Inquiry never leaves Haféz, and he is constantly searching for a pathway to the beloved. Nothing is cast in stone, and there is an evolving rainbow of possibilities. The poet encourages us to continually ask ourselves: Who am I? What am I doing here? And he challenges us not to be dissuaded by half-answers and convenient solutions. We must go all the way, Haféz warns, or we would become prey to every net that is spread to catch us.

For Haféz, his mode of true expression and his livelihood were inseparable. He was a poet who made his living through poetry. Sometimes it may have gained him fame and wealth. At other times it seems to have brought him poverty and condemnation. Either way, he gave up neither his tool of the trade nor the integrity with which he conducted his business. In Haféz, as in any evolved rend, one always finds the impeccability of a warrior who stands by the truth and does not fear loss of reputation or comfort in that integrity. This is the inner nobility of rendi.

In the rend's naturally turbulent spirit, there is a purposeful restfulness, a desire to break through, to experience the unknown, to search for infinite possibilities. The ecstasy is to ride the waves of the turbulent spirit with utmost centeredness, calm, and joy. This is the legacy of Haféz's rend. After all, the poet says, we are surrounded by countless fantasies. Even heavens war with each other. There is danger of deviation in every corner and tangent of the rend's pathway. Be awake, Haféz warns, and maintain your individual freedom.

As humanity races deeper into the dizzying space of the Information Age, with its endless arrays of choices, Haféz pierces our consciousness with a sobering message. To be free, we must stay focused on the singular vision of our unique pathway and not be dissuaded by all the images and external events that come our way. Probe, the poet says; perceive the subtleties and don't be fooled by appearances. Abandon the fantasy of being in control. You are truly in control only if you stay on your true path.

I once wore a coarse woolen cloak to cover my hundred faults;
I pawned it for wine, music, and a forbidden talisman.

The Sufis retrieved all the items they'd pawned for wine;
only my cloak remained in the house of wine seller.

WHEN PASSION WAS BORN

You breathed luster on first day into every cell;
love manifested and the world burned as though Hell.

Your face was revealed but the angels did not see,
so your will became fire to dwell in human shell.

Mind wanted to shape light from this bright flame of love,
but the lightning of ardor reversed the mind's spell.

The seeker sought to see the way through the secrets,
but the swift hand of mystery this stranger did quell.

All others cast their lots to live solely with joy;
only heart and its passion embraced grief as well.

My soul wished to stretch to the dimple of your chin;
so it took journey of curls that rose and then fell.

Haféz wrote the book of the rapture of love's joy
on the day his pen began love's two tales to tell.

Step 5

Focusing Awareness

Your goal is truth, your process is alchemy, and your pathway is rendi. But what can you actually do? What is your technique of learning? Do you sit and meditate? Do you drink red wine bearing the brand name "Shiraz"? Let us explore a brief meditation for getting down to Earth with our poet of wisdom. Imagine that you are sitting in a tavern in Shiraz and you catch sight of a man poised on a corner bench. A cup of wine rests at hand as he talks with friends. Occasionally he takes up his pen and writes a few words. He is at home here. But he is no typical drinker. His eyes are sharp, and he misses nothing that happens in the room. He smiles often. Other patrons obviously know and respect him.

Then it happens. Someone asks the question that is always asked of those who are called "wise":

"What must I do, great teacher, to gain wisdom myself?"

Just as the poet's Elder answers him, so does the poet answer the seeker. He says one word:

"Focus."

"Focus?" asks the seeker. "What does this mean?"

The tavern poet smiles and points to the seeker's eyes. "You have two eyes. Each sees something different. To see the world as it is, you must unite the two images into one. The same is true of your invisible eyes. You have two of these as well. To arrive at wisdom, you must learn what each sees, then unite the two images into one. That is focus."

In "When Passion Was Born," a poem of creation, Haféz explores the origins of his beloved and the futility of trying to understand this process with the mind alone:

Mind wanted to shape light from this bright flame of love,
but the lightning of ardor reversed the mind's spell.

The seeker sought to see the way through the secrets,
but the swift hand of mystery this stranger did quell.

The pathway of the heart took on a special power on the day of creation, however, by embracing grief as well as joy as a stimulus for its response. Thus began the soul's journey to wisdom (as represented, in Persian imagery, by the chin's dimple) through life's up-and-down journey of curls and tangles:

All others cast their lots to live solely with joy;
only heart and its passion embraced grief as well.

My soul wished to stretch to the dimple of your chin;
so it took journey of curls that rose and then fell.

This journey reflects a deep desire to break the boundaries of established order and arrive at an unnamable, yet quite palpable reality of absolute unity. This is a philosophy of growth through mental and spiritual stretching, continuous expansion of the imagination, and living wakefully and well, with your eye focused on beauty. Haféz's own practical tool in expressing and advancing this philosophy is poetry, and his cunning perceptual weapon is biluminosity: recognizing paradox, being fully aware of it every moment, and engaging in a graceful dance with it.

The yearning for unity throws Haféz into a journey of passion and love, pain and despair, disdain and laughter, faithfulness and skepticism. He accepts them all equally. This rendi is synonymous with arrival itself. The pathway witnesses heart-opening break-throughs that often reveal the rewards of rendi, and it culminates in as empowering a rapture as the person walking the pathway desires and is able to absorb. This unified perception is precisely the tool that the tavern poet recommended to the seeker— "Focus."

But this type of focus requires, for most of us anyway, that we shift our perception from paradox to the clarity of unity. If we can create one unified vision of our world rather than a chaotic frame-work of painful choices, then we will have our focus.

Consistent with the concept of unity, process and goal are inseparable in rendi. Paradoxically, you must focus every moment in order to achieve focus. This is also a prime lesson of personal alchemy. You must be a rend at heart, but you also must learn the tools of transforming yourself into a more enlightened form of humanity. The product of this process, the highest essence of the rend's inner being, emerges as both the alchemist and the gold that the alchemist painstakingly draws out of other metals. Like Jam's Cup, it enriches us by bestowing life's wisdom.

As the poet explains in the final lines of "When Passion Was Born":

> *Haféz wrote the book of the rapture of love's joy*
> *on the day his pen began love's two tales to tell.*

This, then, is the lesson both for the seeker in the tavern and for all other potential rends as well. We must learn to know our inner world as clearly as the outer one. And as we proceed on our path and focus our awareness inward, the first thing that comes into clear view is that which creates the core beliefs that condition our lives: our personal mythology.

Chalice or Paradise?

What better than good friends in the garden in spring?
But why should we wait? Why not for cupbearer ring?

Take whatever good times come your way today, dear;
no one can know when the end will come for our fling.

Be aware of the thin thread connecting all life;
though the world suffers on, comfort to yourself bring.

Are not life's elixir and Garden of Eden
the selfsame as this wine and the realm of the king?

The concealed and the drunken are of the same tribe;
which seduction to choose to put heart in a sling?

Hush, sky cannot see the secret under the veil;
O complainer, which choice will appease everything?

If my sins and mistakes are damning transgressions,
we must seek God's mercy for the tiniest sting.

Zahed lusts for Paradise, Haféz seeks the cup;
let us listen for which song God wishes to sing.

Step 6

A Choice of Mythology

As we focus awareness on our individual inner truths, our attention inevitably lands on personal belief systems. For Haféz, the test of one's personal power is the ability to see through that belief system to the point of freeing oneself from outwardly imposed attitudes and reactions. The result of this freedom is that gathered memory begins to assemble itself as an inner replacement for the belief system.

The gathered memory, then, takes on the added dimension of becoming the individual's personal reference system for appropriate responses in daily living. It allows you, the aspiring rend, to observe and judge every situation of your life on its own merits rather than on the basis of some religious or other culturally correct definition of what is right or wrong.

Before that freedom of seeing and choosing can take effect within us, however, the personal belief system—our mythology—must be drawn to our attention. This enables us to understand how detrimental it is to bind ourselves to a rigid and unyielding thought process that allows us to impose expectations, comparisons, and judgments on ourselves and other people. Each of us must reach the point of making a choice as to the content of our personal mythology.

The joyous poem "Chalice or Paradise?" at the start of this chapter deals with precisely this choice. Haféz points out the alternatives in clear terms. He presents himself as a man of the chalice of wine, intoxication, self-seeking, and self-fulfillment. The zahed, in contrast, denies the good times of the moment in order to seek an illusory future Paradise promised in the afterlife to "good" religious followers. The poet makes his own position very clear:

> *Take whatever good times come your way today, dear;*
> *no one can know when the end will come for our fling.*
>
> *Be aware of the thin thread connecting all life;*
> *though the world suffers on, comfort to yourself bring.*

Furthermore, the poet is perfectly willing to let the final judgment rest with the final judge:

> *Zahed lusts for Paradise, Haféz seeks the cup;*
> *let us listen for which song God wishes to sing.*

With Haféz, rendi evolves as a divine intent on Earth. We human beings are here because the Earth itself is a school of alchemy, because this is a temporary place for evolving our souls, because the physical life is a field of learning and growth. This paradigm is radically different from the mythology of sin that permeates the psyche of so much of humanity.

In Islam's myth of creation, Adam and Eve yield to the Devil's temptation and eat five grains of wheat. This results in their banishment from Paradise. This version of the original sin gives rise to a chain of reactions based on guilt, grief, and rejection of the body and its physicality. Alienation such as this destroys the ability to focus on the unity of life. Longing to return the soul to its place of origin, Haféz's zahed engages in rigid rituals and embraces limiting thought forms—the antithesis of the freedom of imagination and expression that constitute the matrix of rendi. As the poet admonishes:

> *Go, zahed, don't invite me to Paradise;*
> *God on first day did not knead me for that place.*

Haféz encourages us to escape the mind-set of original sin and grief and instead put forth a mythology of love and service. Life, Haféz says, is like an overnight stay of a constantly moving caravan. It is meant to be lived to its fullest, with justice, free of plunder, without complaint, but engaged in an uncompromising battle for our right to be free. In this journey, we must laugh at our limitations, seek compatible companions, and take care of our temporary home. He encourages us to focus on and rejoice in the wonder of the universe because we have the capacity to feel love within ourselves and project love toward others. Let's stop mourning over our alienation from Heaven, he says, and let's give up the struggle to attain the fantasy of Paradise:

> *My father sold Eden for just two grains of wheat;*
> *why would I not sell it for one grain of barley?*

The original sin mythology with its theme of the fall of humanity has turned us into whining children who feel that the world owes us everything because Heaven has abandoned us. It has robbed us of our individual and collective senses of responsibility. Let us reverse this mythology, Haféz says, and replace the reactive culture of grief and complaint with the imaginative culture of community.

This revolutionary reversal of focus is at the heart of Haféz's rendi. His dancing and singing poetry inspires us to take charge of our lives, our minds, our psyches, our souls. He invites us to turn grief to joy, instantly, confidently, definitively. Haféz is our voice of consciousness that wants to do something radically different than it has ever done but feels lost in the limitations of its own belief system. Haféz urges us to break the bounds of self-pity and suffering and instead transfer our attention to the more expanded and liberating realms of courage and ecstasy. This is our right to life, and this is the intent of the very spirit that lurks in our hearts and has chosen our bodies as its temporary shelter.

It is in this spirit that Haféz turned from his own contemporary religions to the spiritual insight of ancient Persia. He advises:

Revive the Zoroastrian way in this garden
just as the tulip ignites the magical fire.

The "magical fire" refers to an ancient myth that tells of the patriarch Abraham trying to open the eyes of the Namrud tribe to the true nature of God. When this barbaric tribe resisted his words and lit a fire to burn him as a heretic, God made the fire go cold. There is an ancient way of truth, Haféz is saying, that ran straight from the creative source of God through Abraham and Zarathustra, and that way involves a balance of each being with all of life. Let us look to nature, to the tulip itself, to relax the burning guilt of the fundamentalist's fire.

This is the same attitude expressed in the following passage by George Bernard Shaw:

> This is the true joy of life, the being used for a purpose recognized by yourself as a mighty one ... the being a force of nature instead of a feverish, selfish little clod of ailments and grievances complaining that the world will not devote itself to making you happy.[12]

This also is the outlook that both distinguishes and empowers the traveler of rendi to choose a personal mythology that will inspire life without misleading the mind into futile fantasy.

THE MAGICAL BLINK OF FIRST DAY

My cloak I pawned, fine wine to buy on first day;
absurd book of life drowned in drink of first day.

My whole lifetime I wasted roaming around
while rend's freedom flirted nearby on first day.

While wisdom to servitude a stranger stayed,
my heart-yearning eye blinked a tear on first day.

Zahed's untrue tale I'll not repeat to you;
true song must be played on harp and lyre of first day.

So long as this world travels upside down,
I'll savor cupbearer and cup from first day.

My soul from you will never stray, O sweetheart,
my pain comes from tangled strands of first day.

When you grow old, Haféz, from tavern retire;
rendi and lust are for the young on first day.

Step 7

Inspiration without Fantasy

*L*ike Sheherazad, who buys her life by telling stories to the king for one thousand and one consecutive nights in the classic *Tales of Arabian Nights,* we all possess the capacity for building a life of fantasies. Be aware, says Haféz, be aware. As you begin the alchemical process of revising your mythology, make sure that your gathered memory distinguishes between reality and fantasy.

All the archetypes of the dream world as well as virtually everyone we meet in the material world tell us stories in order to validate their existence. Everyone is trying to mold our minds into the realms of their fantasies. From television advertising to black-cloaked killers chasing us in nightmares, we are surrounded by visions. Our nervous systems gravitate toward anything that awakens the slightest point of familiarity. It may be a cookie or a carnival, but the magnetism of fantasy worlds fills our daily lives.

Awareness of these fantasies is what focus is about. Rather than accepting anyone else's story about the nature of reality, Haféz encourages us to rely on our perceptions. But paradox, of course, is always nearby. At the same time that we condition ourselves not to become lost in fantasy, we must also acknowledge the vital presence of spiritual inspiration.

In "The Magical Blink of First Day," Haféz speaks of pawn-
ing his cloak—probably the woolen Sufi cloak he mentions in
other poems—in order to acquire the fine spiritual wine of "first
day." In Persian literature, "first day" indicates the origin of some-
thing (in this case, life) that actually has no beginning and no end.
Haféz then drowns the "absurd book of life"—the traditionally
accepted stories of humanity's original sin—in that first day's wine.
He reflects on the lifetime he has wasted wandering in fantasy
while the mystical inspiration of "rend's freedom flirted nearby
on first day."

The poem goes on to recall the inspiration of the true wisdom
and song and cup of first day. It declares that this choice between
rendi and obsession with the fantasized appearances of the physical
world and established religion is what life offers to us all in our
youth. Therefore, the wisdom of age should see beyond these temp-
tations, these fantasies:

> *When you grow old, Haféz, from tavern retire;*
> *rendi and lust are for the young on first day.*

While Sheherazad's imagination served her well by saving her
life, the capacity for fantasy deceives most of us in terms of our
spiritual focus. Here again, Haféz emphasizes that we must not
confuse the visible and invisible worlds. Our fantasies of Paradise
and one fundamentalist way of seeing the world may provide
momentary comfort, but they do not create an enduring approach
to reality. In the following couplet, he emphasizes that the search
for comfort is not the rend's purpose:

> *Luxury of comfort is no bridge to beloved,*
> *for loving is the path of the painstaking rend.*

Simply by living, we already are questing for meaning in life.
Whether we acknowledge it or not, moment-to-moment and
day-to-day existence thrusts itself forward through the cycling
process of our seasons and ages. We travel as passengers, guests of
existence amid its ever-changing scenarios. We watch the world

go by the windows of our senses. If we are willing to look past these scenarios without being tempted by the comforts offered and caught up in their tangles, rendi offers itself as a potential alternative pathway.

Like everyone else, rends cannot blank out their inner voices. They cannot totally shut out the passing scenes that impress their sensory images on our nervous systems as sights and sounds and tastes and smells and feelings. We process these sensations and then we respond, often in a way so subtle we're not even aware of it. Simultaneously, in our mental mechanisms, we register the history of our individual processes of sensory intake and response. This is how we start thinking:

> *Treasured visions from soul transcend my mental space;*
> *prepare your mind to grasp these tones vital to grace.*

To whatever degree our sensory tools make known to our conscious minds the intricacies of our personal processes, we also are capable of reflecting on them. We reflect in order to expand our perception of what is happening within and around us. This reflecting, this search for meaning, is mentality in action. It can go on forever. We reflect on the reflections of our reflections until our minds are filled with a spiraling chain of self-generated images, each carrying its own sensory reactions—including emotions. In time, these emotions become spontaneously combustible within our mentality. Our minds become little furnaces with fires of rage and fear burning, just waiting to burst up into conscious expression as our reactions to recurring mental images.

What started as a simple quest for meaning bogs down in a quagmire of intellectualism. The problem with all this reflective activity is that it tends to obscure the sensations of existence that inspired our original responses and thoughts. As a result, our mentality develops a deep-seated tendency to avoid direct perception of existence in its most basic form. We end up in denial of our original nature because of our mentality, the very tool that enables us to understand that we have an original nature. But even thinking about this problem is a mental process that tempts us into more reflection. Reflection builds on reflection.

The way to short-circuit all this reflection and its end result of obfuscation of the true nature of existence, the mystic philosophy of Haféz proclaims, is to acknowledge the existence of spiritual inspiration as a necessary attribute of rendi. Such inspiration—the direct experience of life force—is always there, the poet says, and it offers knowledge and wisdom. But we have to want it:

> *This cup of wine urges mind to flee its narrow scope;*
> *the gate to the invisible looms just beyond your hope.*

Spiritual inspiration offers us, as seekers, an alternative to the never-ending process of reflection on reflections. It is rather like having the opportunity to buy direct from the producer rather than getting caught up trying to figure out which retailer offers the best deal. We get a fresher product at a lower cost.

Spiritual inspiration also provides an alternative method of responding to the sensations registered by our nervous systems. Instead of getting stuck in the pattern of reactions that includes reflection, obfuscation, and denial, we are offered instantaneous perception and identification of reality. Haféz describes this process as the state of intoxication or drunkenness—the losing of one's mind and its limited view. And he recommends it highly. Only through intoxication, he declares over and over, can the rend reach the beloved. Only then can we transcend the control that mentality and its derivative reflections assert over us. This transcendence involves our coming face to face with the spirit in a state of intoxication and then soberly identifying what we see. This capacity, he says, is always with us:

> *Your love is my being, and your kindness in my heart*
> *is mixed with my essence, to depart only at death.*

Our need to consciously acknowledge and embrace spiritual presence in our everyday lives is as important now as it was for Haféz in fourteenth-century Persia. While he balanced his own perceptions in an atmosphere of Mongol conquerors threatening Shiraz and local shahs and mullahs objecting to the truths of his poetry, the modern world offers its own dehumanizing threats that we constantly are tempted to shovel into our furnaces of reflection.

Simply acknowledging the presence of spiritual inspiration in our lives is an important step in rendi. Whether our minds are in touch with this spirituality all the time, part of the time, or not at all, it is still there. We can always look to our hearts and find a different message than that projected onto us by the outside world.

When They Made Me into Who I Am

Angels knocked in my night dream at the tavern door;
wine steeped with Adam's clay in my cup they did pour.

These visitors from the secret harems on high
shared sweetness with me down on my lower world floor.

Love's blessings overran sky's unlimited space;
my intoxication the lottery did score.

Forgive seventy-two nations for going to war;
they lost their clear vision by believing false lore.

Thank God there is peace between beloved and me;
with this dancing and drinking, her lies I'd adore.

If I could not see danger in the candle flame,
fire would burn butterfly's fearless wings to their core.

Since the very first time pens combed the curls of words,
only Haféz alone unmasks truth evermore.

Step 8

Clarity in Ecstasy

*T*he teachings of the school of alchemy balance spiritual inspi-
ration with an insistence on clear thinking. Ecstasy and logic are
both close friends of Haféz. In the poem "When They Made Me
into Who I Am," Haféz emphasizes the need for seeing clearly in
the midst of intoxication. While he is immersed in the ecstasy of
loving angels whose "blessings overran sky's unlimited space," he
sees the dangers inherent in his mind's lack of judgment in this
condition:

> *Thank God there is peace between beloved and me;*
> *with this dancing and drinking, her lies I'd adore.*
>
> *If I could not see danger in the candle flame,*
> *fire would burn butterfly's fearless wings to their core.*

Furthermore, he sees how this inability to distinguish between
true and false information can affect us on many levels:

> *Forgive seventy-two nations for going to war;*
> *they lost their clear vision by believing false lore.*

Still, the poet remains confident in his own perception:

Since the very first time pens combed the curls of words,
only Haféz alone unmasks truth evermore.

From this perspective of spiritually inspired clear thinking and focus, Haféz presents his own vividly perceived dilemma of survival in a world of distractions. How can I hope to struggle through a vast expanse of tempting fantasies with a clear mind, the poet asks in the following couplet, when even Adam succumbed to Eve's temptation of only a little wheat?

How do I walk safe through fantasy fields
where we harvest all our schemes and our pain?

Remember Father Adam, guileless and pure,
surrendered his mind to just one single grain.

As with so many of Haféz's assertions, however, biluminosity peers through the complaint and converts it into a declaration of the potential of personal destiny. If we do not assume that Haféz wants to survive temptation, then the fact that Adam "surrendered his mind" does not become a disastrous event for all future humankind. Losing one's mind stands as a metaphor for accessing spiritual awakening, thereby allowing the rend to avoid the denial of safely walking through life unaware.

From this perspective of deeper meaning, Eve and her feminine energy turn from villains into heroines in our basic mythology. But seeing this potential requires a mentality capable of cutting through the surface fantasy that before surrendering to material temptation, Adam was leading a blissfully innocent utopian existence pleasurable beyond the dreams of mortal humanity and, further, that this innocence is the most highly desirable condition for us all.

For Haféz, clear thought refers to the ability to avoid the tempting fantasies of outer allurements that offer grandiose and unrealistic visions. We must understand that the more enduring values dwell within and that no temptation of short-term thrills in the outer world is worth surrendering our inner focus. Still, we must also grant that the capacity to be productive in the physical world can enhance the environment in which we pursue spiritual experience. But if we confuse the two worlds and the realities each offers, we begin to develop neuroses:

The savants are the center of life's compass,
but love knows that they are lost in its circle.

Understanding the concerns and limits of our inner and outer worlds, then, is the purpose of clear thought. It allows us to avoid futile actions inspired by fantasies. The clearer our thinking, the more powerful our focus for considering, deciding on, and implementing courses of productive action in daily life. Spiritual inspiration, when not balanced by mental groundedness that guides us in discerning between the worlds of visible and invisible forms, contains a potentially obsessive aspect that can turn us into its victims rather than its partners in perception.

We can achieve clear thinking by first acknowledging that we see and/or hear before we think. In other words, perception—not reflection—is our most immediate source of clarity. We must learn to trust the instinctual nature of our most primordial inner source of wisdom. Then we use our mental focus to apply that inner wisdom in its most appropriate form to the outer world. Clarity divides the spiritual and logical aspects of life, but it does not value one over the other. The ultimate purpose of this division is unity, which can be achieved only when the complementary aspects of both sides are well defined. Then they become compatible, and eventually as user-friendly as a computer's interfacing hardware and software.

Were Haféz to appear suddenly on the contemporary spiritual scene, we would find no greater critic or opponent of the current cults that demand that their members surrender to the will of their leaders. Haféz is an individualist, a focused freethinker who sees the surrendering of one's will to religious conformity as an ultimate violation of one's deepest aspect of humanity. Sacrifice neither inner nor outer life, he stresses. Do not compromise on this matter. The clear pathway of humanity is to embrace all that can be seen rather than to deny any part of it.

Haféz embraces both spiritual and mental clarity throughout

his writing. His poetry sings about, acts out, and dances to the many complex melodies and interweavings of the symphony of life. His inclusiveness seems to grow out of the style of Saadi, a popular ghazal master who lived and wrote in Shiraz about half a century earlier. Unlike most other Persian poets, Saadi concentrated his verse on worldly rather than otherworldly relationships. As Haféz developed his own ghazal style, he blended Saadi's grounded worldliness with the more ecstatic concerns of Rumi and others. As a result, Haféz's poetry resounds as a symphony of both worlds. He is inspired by the ecstatic music of the spheres, and he is as thoughtful as a scholar studying geometry or logic. His capacity for blending these elements into a personal viewpoint while spicing them thoroughly with mythology and mysticism creates his unique mystique among Persian poets.

Perhaps the most telling application of Haféz's clear thinking about distinguishing the visible and invisible worlds involves his description of the rend's stance in regard to prophecy, a position that he addresses in a number of poems. The rend, he declares, is a spiritual person. The rend is someone who, through direct contact with the other side, embodies the message of the world of spirit. The rend sees the whole of humanity's condition and understands the source of both suffering and ecstasy.

But the rend does not ever claim to be a prophet. This is a prime demonstration of the ultimate application of clear thinking. As a human being in the material world, the rend never takes the position of being the primary personal source of the Creator's message to the rest of humanity. Such a position plants a field of fantasy with far too great a possibility for yielding obsession and self-deception—far too much grain for Haféz's taste. And besides, delivering prophecy is an untenable position for the rend because rendi also is about having the compassion to allow others to choose their own pathway. In the final analysis, it's quite simple:

> *I possess no sound sweeter than the song of love,*
> *that eternal melody orbiting this dome.*

THE SCENT OF KINDNESS

Nightingale sang to flower as dawn did creep:
In this garden, flowers like you are quite cheap.

Flower laughed and replied: True words cannot harm
but a lover who hurts, her love will not keep.

If you want to drink wine from that jeweled cup,
on your lashes string gently pearls from the deep.

Kindness' scent will never awaken the senses
of that one whose cheek does not tavern floor sweep.

At Eram Garden last night a soft breeze rose
and the hyacinth fell when the wind turned steep.

I asked Jam: What became of your globe-wise cup?
He said: Awakened people went back to sleep.

If word of love is not that which flows from lips,
cupbearer, pour wine before angst makes us weep.

Haféz, your tears cast reason far out to sea,
leaving anguish of love its own pain to reap.

Step 9

The Gift of Compassion

Compassion is respect for all beings' pathways. Acknowledging one's own spiritual nature is relatively easy. Accepting that everyone else—and everything else—embodies that same spirit is a bit more of a challenge. But if we can do so, we will have no desire to impose our personal pathway on anyone else. We also do not desire to control another's experiences, because the individual must engage in his or her unique journey. This is another prime lesson in the school of alchemy.

As a result of granting this sacred space to others, judgment and comparison and expectation of others are suspended. This concept is reflected in the old saying included in the cultural aphorisms of most peoples on Earth: Don't criticize another until you've walked a mile in that person's shoes. In "The Scent of Kindness," Haféz says:

> *Kindness' scent will never awaken the senses*
> *of that one whose cheek does not tavern floor sweep.*

Developing compassion engenders understanding, tolerance, patience, and a refusal to accept your own being as either limited to one physical body or ceasing to exist when your personal lifetime ends. You are part of all existence, and in some way or other all existence flows through you as well. This understanding is central to rendi.

Haféz speaks often of the rend's capacity for feeling the pain of the world and taking that pain and using it to bridge the gap between the suffering self and the healing love of the invisible unknown. Rends, he says, are the generators of the natural essence of infinity. They are the stretchers of humanity's envelope—and compassion is a great tool for stretching. Mystery sends rends into this existence for the very purpose of fulfilling this role, which, in turn, stretches the rend as well:

> *Since becoming the bondsman of love's tavern door,*
> *each moment a new sadness congratulates me.*

Compassion transports us to the realization that whatever affects the world at large also affects the individual. In this context, pain is seen as separation, the action of internally splitting apart. Whether it is a single atom splitting, or the earth hurting, or humanity crying out, the act of separation is accompanied by a cry for help that is heard by the universe. This cry is of a yearning for reunion of the parts that have separated. This, of course, is the longing quality that permeates Persian poetry—the desire to heal the pain of the universe through reunion with the beloved.

Healing by taking on the pain of another person or of the world itself corresponds to the wounded healer function of shamanic cultures. Tribal shamans around the world have practiced their arts for many centuries while observing the principle that they themselves must first have suffered and recovered from whatever affliction they are attempting to cure. The immunity built up by their own experience protects them from being victimized by the pain of their patients. Unaffected and unafraid, they project their own images of recovery into the patients' processes:

> *I showed my bloody tears to the doctors who said:*
> *It is love's pain, but a burning heart can be healed.*

Buddha reached enlightenment by meditating on the pain he saw in the world: the sickness, aging, and death of his fellow humans. In Christianity, Jesus is said to have healed the afflicted by taking on the burden of their sins. Such processes reflect the interrelatedness of all things within the web of existence. This concept of unity among all people, all beings, and all creation has been the central theme of all major religions since Zarathustra initiated the concept of a single deity as the basis of his teachings in ancient Persia.

During intoxication, the rend becomes aware of the constant condition of the pain of the splitting of existence—the literal ripping apart of unity—but also the corresponding constant condition of reunion. The pain comes in when the rend realizes that most of humanity feels only the splitting, not the reuniting, and therefore uses most of its mental energy to reflect on this image of painful separation. Projecting the mental image of reunion to humanity during intoxication becomes one of the rend's methods of healing the world's pain. As a poet, Haféz uses his artistry to convey the message of unity to us in a manner that penetrates our visible world as well as the invisible:

Although intoxication shattered me, I know
that my own foundation rests in that shatteredness.

Compassion as an integral element of rendi does not, however, promote feelings of pity for others, self-pity, guilt, or helplessness. We can identify a condition while refusing to identify *with* that condition, but a fine shade of perception is required. Distinguishing between true compassion and the feeling that results in looking down on others and feeling sorry for them can be illustrated by examining the two different kinds of selfishness. One type of selfishness is greedy, unsharing—the opposite of unselfishness; the second type of selfishness is the reverse of selflessness—having a strong sense of who you are. In the first case, compassion is not present; in the second case, knowing one's inner nature becomes synonymous with practicing compassion.

For Haféz, daily survival at times demanded a finely honed

talent in statesmanship and diplomacy. Being able to see a situation from a viewpoint contradictory to your own is at the heart of success in this type of endeavor. To see and feel what your opponent sees and feels can open a pathway into a unified solution to any dispute:

> *If price of union with you is my life, I will buy;*
> *the clear-sighted buy quality, no matter the cost.*

This application of compassion finds many contemporary opportunities in today's personal, business, and international relations. To feel the feelings of your lover without being obsessed by reactions to them; to understand that an appropriate business transaction means profit for all involved; and to realize that violence and warmongering are, without exception, divisive rather than unifying pathways—all these are examples of applied compassion.

OF WILL AND IMMORTALS

They came just before dawn, as in grief I did plead;
I drank life's elixir and watched darkness recede.

They turned me ecstatic in the brightness of soul,
gave me wine from cup of the awakening seed.

Such a blessed dawn and such a time to rejoice—
that moment divine they handed down my fresh deed.

Henceforth I'll search mirror of beloved's image
where they did appear and my new essence decreed.

I'm cheered, it's no mystery my desires are fulfilled;
they found me worthy and my starvation did feed.

That angelic voice told me of riches to come
through patience in the face of suffering and need.

All this sweetness and nectar that flow from my words
are enduring rewards given me by that weed.

Through the will of Haféz and souls of immortals
emerges liberation—from slavery I'm freed.

Step 10

Generosity's Impulse

*G*enerosity springs from a complete, concentrated, passionate impulse to participate in manifesting in concrete reality that which you feel possesses a strong, yet unknown potential. You therefore embrace the unknown and intend it to become known. Then you forget about it. You do not look back. This meaning of generosity extends our lessons in the school of alchemy, and it also illustrates the subtle power that accumulates to the rend through the qualities of the gathered memory. The more you are aware of your true and complete metaphysical nature, the more you can influence the world around you.

Generosity, as a quality of rendi, is the other side of compassion. While compassion decrees that you do not force your own pathway onto other people, generosity requires you to offer your gifts to the world for any traveler who passes by. And this offer is made freely, with no expectation of reward or payment. This is a special kind of giving, an act that you permit rather than perform. You declare, in essence, that an inherent obligation to the life that you inhabit is to allow your own creative forces the range and freedom to affect whatever they happen to touch. For Haféz, the beauty of Shiraz's roses and the call of the nightingales exemplify the generosity of nature, the type of generosity he suggests we emulate.

Hafez has chronicled the generosity of his own spirit guides and angels in "Of Will and Immortals." Scholars say that this poem is the story of a forty-day vigil that resulted in his discovering his own genius for poetry. He opens the poem by rejoicing in his ecstatic awakening from drinking the intoxicating elixir of life. This awakening leads to his receiving a new life's "deed"— a document issued in old Persia to indicate that a debt had been paid in full:

> Such a blessed dawn and such a time to rejoice—
> that moment divine they handed down my fresh deed.

Having found the poet worthy of receiving the gift that he sought from spirit, the predawn visitors explained that their generosity was a reward for his "patience in the face of suffering and need." His new deed had its roots in both his own will and in the beneficence of the spirit:

> Through the will of Hafez and souls of immortals
> emerges liberation—from slavery I'm freed.

Desiring no credit for the gifts you give can be a more active effort than the actual giving. But the act of allowing life to proceed without asking it to heap praise on our efforts can be an empowering experience. The best gifts are those with no strings, and there is no better example of this than the guidance given in Hafez's *Divan,* one of the world's popular tools for divination.

Centuries of spiritual seekers would undoubtedly consider Hafez a supreme practitioner of generosity for all the guidance and support bestowed by his poetry. Furthermore, his work meets rendi's criteria for generosity: His poetry sprang from an impulse to manifest unknown potential from spirit into thought; he allowed his work to take whatever form was necessary for it to serve humanity in the best possible way; and he certainly did not expect any reward, for he could not have known he was creating this particular gift.

Haféz did not collect his own poems into a book, and he undoubtedly did not intend them to be used for divination. Scholars gathered the poems following his death. Today in Iran, there are many different versions of the *Divan,* and each editor creates a new assortment with altered versions of poems, some of which are attributed rather questionably to Haféz.

Still, despite this lack of a unified agreement about the form and content of the book, uncounted readers have been able to decipher its counsel and comfort over the centuries. They ask a question, open the book, read a poem, and perhaps also consult the next poem as the "witness"—or *shahed*—that clarifies or expands the first. Often, as has been reported in many previous books, advice of great clarity emerges. It seems wondrous that today, so many centuries after the poet lived and wrote, seekers with pure hearts and open minds can access Haféz's guidance with startling accuracy through any organization of the *Divan.*

All this guidance through divination—and also through simply reading and feeling the beautiful and insightful poetry—is unquestionably a great gift from Haféz. His application of the metaphysical mechanics of universal mysticism to personal observations about his own culture set the stage for centuries of wisdom transmissions through the *Divan.* He wrote his poetry and left it for the world to do with as it pleased, and the result has been an appreciation he could never have anticipated.

Something Haféz did intend, however, was to distinguish between generosity and humility. In generosity, there is no discounting of your deserving rewards when they are offered. There is no self-sacrifice. Yet there is also almost a devil-may-care attitude toward the world's reaction to whatever you may do. You simply do your best, give freely of whatever creativity or energy you may command, and enjoy life's procession. Public acclaim simply cannot be the yardstick by which you measure yourself. The rend is free of such concerns, focusing instead on spiritual feeling, consistently clear thinking, and spiritual inspiration. Only this type of concentration frees the inner creativity and artistry of any human being. Profit and loss become irrelevant.

All this sounds fine, we speculate, but would Haféz advise this approach as a philosophy for starting or growing a business venture, whether in his own century or today? After all, we are a culture built on the principle of making profit and avoiding loss. And Haféz himself is far from a dreamy-eyed artist. His writing yields advice on economics as well as artistry, so how does he balance the need for prosperity with the attribute of generosity?

It is really very simple. Life is about doing, he stresses, whether you are an artist or a merchant. Judge no one, and focus on your own unique pathway, market position, or niche. Have a clear vision of your potential, but do not enclose your performance within a fence of expectations that limits your full expression of that potential. Conduct your daily deals, write your poetry at night, do whatever you do, but do it in the spirit of giving your own gifts to the world. Generosity is an inner feeling. No matter what your personal situation, you still can feel generous toward the rest of the world. Generosity is a description of your attitude toward life, not a command to give your money away. But generosity as an attitude can, in time, also be profitable.

Embodying generosity, you see, attracts generosity toward you from all other beings. It works like a magnet, just as your own smile elicits smiles from others. In order to attract prosperity, you let go of the desire to be rewarded for every little thing you do. Develop the feeling of being generous, of giving. Forget the price tags on your talents. The world is full of its own generosity and offers rewards and gifts far beyond your imagination. So, do your work, do it well for its own sake, do not be concerned about short-term rewards, and open yourself up to life's full and extraordinary capacity for generosity toward you. It's a completely natural process, declares the poet. Just observe the universe itself, as it continuously bestows the gift of generosity:

When the spring cloud felt the drought of the season,
its tears fell on jasmine, hyacinth, and jonquil.

When West Wind heard Haféz's verse from nightingale,
it touched sweet basil and spread beauty tranquil.

BLESSINGS IN THE SNARES

For falling in love I am the talk of the town;
I, whom fantasy cannot deceive or drag down.

With my wine-worshiping I sought truth that's unknown,
so my self-worshiping in that ocean would drown.

I'll keep faith despite critics and happy I'll be,
for suffering is sin on this path of renown.

Elder, I asked: How from myself do I flee?
As he raised cup he said: Secrets reveal a crown.

Learn from beloved the way of kindness and flow;
the circle of beauty will bring joy to your frown.

What is your intent in observing world's garden
if not to love flowers like your eye's iris brown?

Let's to tavern return now from this assembly,
free of all hypocrites who in world do abound.

Just know there are blessings in the snares of beloved;
without all these tangles, how could life spin around?

Haféz, kiss wine cups and beloved's lips only,
but not abstinence preacher, that sin-selling clown.

Step 11

The Need for Stretching

*H*aving reached the halfway point of our journey of rendi, we now can understand that this pathway is a process parallel to the school of alchemy. To study inner alchemy is to travel the worldly path of changing our thinking and our behavior. The result of both processes is to increase the power of the gathered memory. To travel rendi is to expand the mind, to focus on awareness of the big picture of life at all times. Mind expansion is about fearlessness, about being willing and able to stretch and embrace new and different realities. As the mind ceases its compulsive desire to reactively judge whatever it comes into contact with, we learn to accept rather than reject paradox.

In Middle Eastern linguistics, this concept is expressed by *seé sadr,* a literary phrase derived from Arabic. It literally means "expanded chest." In terms of Haféz, this translates into a wider breadth of perspective or perception. Seé sadr also describes the particular stance of broad-mindedness in its eternal war against narrow-mindedness.

Rendi offers a definite opening into the generosity of mind expansion, an opening that prescribes doing away with obsessive self-concern. Haféz writes in "Blessings in the Snares":

With my wine-worshiping I sought truth that's unknown
so my self-worshiping in that ocean would drown.

As often happens, though, Elder must be consulted:

Elder I asked: How from myself do I flee?
As he raised cup he said: Secrets reveal a crown.

Learn from beloved the way of kindness and flow;
the circle of beauty will bring joy to your frown.

And furthermore, make a practice of seeing potential in what first
appears to be negative:

Just know there are blessings in the snares of beloved;
without all these tangles, how could life spin around?

But, it is stressed, concentrate on the clarity of ecstasy and your
passion for freedom; do not fall in love with the paralyzing mes-
sage of the fundamentalist:

Haféz, kiss wine cups and beloved's lips only,
but not abstinence preacher, that sin-selling clown.

For Haféz, the war of broad-mindedness against narrow-
mindedness meant a war against the zaheds and their religious
hypocrisy.

Life, the poet warns, is filled with seemingly honest people
who say one thing and mean another. They put on a public face
that reflects what they believe others want to see, not what is
truly inside them. These are dangerous, misleading people who
distort truth. Their minds are so narrow that they see only the
thin pathway of self-interest to travel. And they want to control
others to such a degree that they refuse to acknowledge that other
paths even exist.

Haféz's poetry was his weapon in the war against hypocrisy.
In verse after verse, he warns his readers about the religious lead-
ers in their fancy robes and the spiritual shallowness of those who
conduct public ceremonies in order to demonstrate their own
wisdom.

Ask only rends about the secrets of the veil;
the honored zaheds are in no mood to answer.

It might seem at first glance that taking such a strong position is not a demonstration of an expanded mind at all. Does it not involve a one-sided view of Haféz's public opponents? Is he not judging them? If mind expansion is about embracing paradox, why does Haféz not show generosity and compassion toward his enemies?

Aha, Haféz answers this assertion, this is the problem of confusing the two worlds again. Personal alchemy is about the inner world, about the qualities we wish to develop in order to know who we are. When we have developed these qualities and established them as cornerstones of our being, we become rends, capable of taking uncompromising stands on significant issues in day-to-day life.

Rendi's demand that we not judge others means that we must maintain our inner integrity, that we not allow thoughts about someone else's goodness or badness to pull us away from concentration on our own direct contact with spiritual inspiration or the clarity of our thinking. The result of being centered in ourselves gives us the courage and, in fact, creates the demand that we take clear stands on the issues of our outer world. Mind expansion means not condoning political or business practices that create public images of goodness while bringing about private detrimental effects. It also means standing up for public standards supporting the integrity of human interaction in terms of justice and unity.

In terms of Haféz and his war, we can observe that it was the mental expansion of his own rendi that allowed him to stand back and gauge the nature of his enemies so that he could describe them with great accuracy. His public stance took on the purpose of telling the truth as it appears to someone who examines all sides of a question and who has no hidden agenda in interpreting and revealing that truth. As a result, his writing—a declaration against hypocrisy—has stood for centuries as a demonstration of ingenious accuracy about political, social, and spiritual affairs.

Letting go of personal judgment about another does not mean suspending the capacity to observe and describe truth:

Zahed's pride yields no healthy conclusion;
rend, by contrast, flies straight to beloved.

As a matter of fact, it is this very quality of being able to see and then report the nature of a wide vision of our existence that we identify with those we consider to possess true genius. Haféz could see the power of such vision in poets such as Rumi and Saadi. He understood what Pythagoras brought to the world in his mathematics and what Plato expressed in philosophy. Certainly he would hold himself to no lesser standard. Haféz's war against hypocrisy has endured and today emerges as a universal demand for social justice, freedom, and individual rights. Meanwhile, the publicly pious clergy of the fourteenth century have evolved into today's self-serving politicians and public leaders who build up private fortunes at the expense of those they purportedly serve.

But mind expansion is about more than just this war. It is about experiencing the pleasure of being willing to delve into direct experience. As Haféz says many times, opposing hypocrisy demands the seeking of pleasure and good times. Otherwise, when we open ourselves to embrace our opponents, we would be overcome by their small-mindedness. Our own inner position must embody enough joy to allow us to remain focused and motivated.

This joy comes from standing in the position of broad-mindedness, where no walls of fear or self-interest shut down our vision. Viewing our lives from this position, we realize the gift and limitations of our mortality. We see that existence is an adventure of such magnitude that its essence cannot be expressed except through our desire to continually broaden the vision itself. Thus, as Haféz takes his uncompromising stand against hypocrisy, he also expresses the more expansive view of the deeper reality:

My persecutor has no faults, my enemy no blame;
like me, in secret dreams they search for the infinite flame.

A Tale of Love

In the garden at dawn I sought for a rose
when nightingale's voice broke the peace with her prose.

Like me, she was mad for love of a flower
and woke up the garden by trilling her woes.

I strolled round the garden moment by moment,
eyeing songbird's affair with flower she chose.

Sweet flower did swoon while the nightingale wooed;
this one's yet to age, that one's caught in love's throes.

As nightingale's song penetrated my heart,
it erased all desires my mind could compose.

In garden where so many roses abound,
to pick even one is to learn where thorn grows.

Haféz, seek no comfort from life's wheel turning,
for its one thousand squeaks create no repose.

Step 12

The Rage of Love

*D*eclaring that Persian poetry is about love is rather like saying that wineglasses are used for wine. In both cases, the vessel draws its existence from the essence that flows within. In terms of rendi, love is a volatile presence, a voluptuous purpose, and an inevitable longing for reunion with the beloved. Both divine and human love fuel the condition of one-heartedness, and both reflect the most profound feelings of intoxication.

As the rend balances spirituality and mentality to cultivate compassion and generosity, mental expansion takes up its protective stance against the threatened incursion of narrow-mindedness. In turn, another process must also arise to assure that the inner war generated by broad-mindedness does not spill over into outer life as a harshly expressed resistance against the world's offerings of experience and emotion. Our desire for love is this insurance against the rend's shutting down the world of feelings.

In "A Tale of Love," Haféz reports on watching a nightingale and rose act out his own desire for the heart of the beloved. As usual in his verses, the love may be seen as either worldly or ethereal:

In the garden at dawn I sought for a rose
when nightingale's voice broke the peace with her prose.

But this desire called love is far from peaceful for the one who does the loving:

Like me, she was mad for love of a flower
and woke up the garden by trilling her woes.

Watching bird and flower, the poet realizes that the exchange between lovers involves a number of different feelings and patterns of behavior. Love is not a simple, easily understood feeling:

Sweet flower did swoon while the nightingale wooed;
this one's yet to age, that one's caught in love's throes.

Finally, the painful side of love becomes as evident as the desirable side. In the end, we get the message that there's no comfort in love. But remember, too, as Haféz stresses, rendi is not about comfort:

In garden where so many roses abound,
to pick even one is to learn where thorn grows.

Haféz, seek no comfort from life's wheel turning,
for its one thousand squeaks create no repose.

In order to be a truly desirable pathway, rendi must embrace the full range of feelings that we can experience. Within that range, the desperation stemming from separation from the beloved emerges as the most powerful entity for Haféz and the other poets in his lineage. For five hundred years, Rudaki and Khayyam and Rumi had been calling from their depths for divine spiritual reunion. Then came Saadi in Shiraz, just before Haféz. In Saadi's writing, the ghazal turned into a love song to be sung on Earth about the beings of the Earth. Informed by these two approaches, Haféz opened his mental arms and wrote of both spiritual and worldly aspects of love.

Love as the craving for this unity is the attribute of rendi that inspires the expansion of our beings. In today's terminology, such love stretches our envelopes. As Haféz writes:

> *For lovers alone this Earth spins up to speed;*
> *to feel no love is to lack the true rend's seed.*

The true rend, remember, is Haféz himself, the unorthodox spiritual seeker. Love, divine or otherwise or all-inclusive, is the motivating force at any given moment. In the verse just quoted, the true rend is distinguished from the profane debauchee who stumbles through life without purpose. That lack of purpose is the lack of love.

The goal of rendi can be defined as the state of inner unity, the condition of completion, the gathered memory. That quality can also be called, quite simply, love. For Haféz, achieving this unity gives meaning to all the rest of existence, and this is an accomplishment worth any risk, any cost. Here is how he explains it:

> *Certain things fulfill us, seduce us to stay;*
> *a thought of hand's touch on her face becomes sweet.*
>
> *A blossom needs the beloved's reflection;*
> *cypress and flower with a song are replete.*
>
> *This body is a particle—there's no fun*
> *or fulfillment until surrender's complete.*

In this final verse, we find perhaps the greatest secret of all: Love is surrender. The surrender of ourselves, our bodies, everything. Only then does the possibility of true completion arise as the essence of love. And, the poet says, this is our natural state, so why fight it?

> *Since eternity, love's been my destiny;*
> *this inscribed fate cannot be erased from me.*

THE END OF DESIRE

She who finds silence does not wandering desire;
so why desert journeys do you desire?

Dear one, midst the yearnings you thrust out to God,
stop for a moment, ask what you desire.

O blessings-giver, rising forged from grief's flame,
ask yourself, what does this pauper desire?

We are masters of yearning, not of insight;
when giving arrives you shall not desire.

If you want to possess life, don't moralize,
just plunder on 'til you do not desire.

The friend's pure heart tells the same tale as Jam's Cup,
reflecting those needs you will not desire.

Gone are the days I sought help from the sailor;
gaining the pearl, the sea you'll not desire.

O poor lover, when the friend's life-giving lips
become yours to kiss, you will not desire.

O seeker, leave me, there's no more to say;
friends abound and foes we never desire.

Silence, Haféz, art and knowledge will suffice;
to dispute our souls is not our desire.

Step 13

Surrender to Mystery

*T*he surrender of physical desire into the more profound unity of divine love arouses an inner relaxation that we call tranquillity. This relaxation carries with it the knowledge that our deepest personal condition is more profoundly connected with the vast invisible world of spirit than with the limited phenomenal outer world. This condition is also known as the gathered memory.

Rendi encourages our continuous acknowledgment of the presence of a tranquillity that lies behind our chattering minds, beyond our repetitious syndromes of behavior. Neither fear nor anger can disengage it from our beings. Tranquillity is the great sea of consistency within our hearts. It can be difficult to access at times, but it is the abode of a great secret that we seek every day of our lives:

> *As for us, kindred friends, all molded from one clay,*
> *our fragile peace of mind must be reshaped each day.*

One of the measures of Haféz's rend is awareness of the hidden treasure of knowledge deep within the sea of tranquillity. Although it is secluded within the inner world, this knowledge directly affects the way we look at and understand our life in the

outer world. It offers us freedom from the seriousness of our ev-
eryday activities.

Intoxication through the spiritual entryway of our choice brings
us into contact with this knowledge. If we meditate, we follow
the path of our own breathing until the surface emotions and
thoughts quiet down. Then the sea of tranquillity appears. We
continue to follow our breathing into the sea itself. Our intoxica-
tion takes over, and, either through silent voice or in some other
profound manner, the knowledge begins to reveal itself to us:

A star shone and became the Moon of this gathering;
it became friend and confidant of my fearful heart.

The essence of the message of knowledge is that the sea in
which we currently exist—the meditative waters of tranquillity—
is an ongoing flow. The phenomenal world, by contrast, is a mo-
mentary image that we have conjured up to challenge us into
expanding our capacity for perception and response. We may con-
jure our planet and our bodies into existence, and we may believe
that they represent the limits of life, but conjuring and believing
do not create truth. At the depth of intoxication, we find the
height of our being, that part of ourselves that is not subject to
the disease and destruction of the outer world.

The implications of this discovery affect our attitudes about
how we live in the outer world. Understanding that all aspects of
physical existence are ephemeral, we no longer take it all so seri-
ously. In time, we realize the futility of tying up our personal
identities with the names and roles assigned to us. Ambition and
striving become comical as our primary motivations. Personal
advancement ceases to excite us in our innermost beings.

We realize that in a few thousand or perhaps million years, the
land on which we walk and the homes in which we live could all
be under water. The books we read and write will have disinte-
grated into tiny particles of dust. The names we work so hard to
make for ourselves will disappear from the records and sounds of
existence. Our planet, a small whirling speck within the immea-

surable vastness of our cosmos, lives a precarious existence, and we are very small beings on this planet. Why, we must ask ourselves in the light of this viewpoint, do we struggle so mightily to accomplish and achieve transitory victories and temporary rewards?

Were we to experience this revelation during our everyday state of mind, we might plunge into the depths of depression and neuroses. But in the gathered memory of the sea of tranquillity, these perceptions actually become inspirational realizations. They come to us in a biluminous manner, the upside of released desire lighting up the downside of physical impermanence.

This surrender to mystery invites the sea of tranquillity to transcend our mental concepts of the beginning and end of existence. Tranquillity is a product of unity, of the biluminous opening and closing of the very heart of existence from which we as human beings flow and to which we return. Our capacity to retain this realization as we return from intoxication to daily life determines our effectiveness in improving our personal situation by becoming nonreactive to the physical world. As Haféz writes:

> *I spin the wheel of life but if it turns not my way,*
> *I will not be weakened by fates of Heaven and Earth.*

After we are touched by the knowledge of our transitory physicality amid the greater sea of existence, we realize that our daily tasks and troubles are no longer matters of life and death. We still do our best and perform our work as well as possible. But the daily grind tends to lose its heaviness and to surrender the control it previously maintained over our lives. The transition is a freeing experience. In the words attributed to Socrates by Plato, "That person is happiest who is content with the least, for content is the wealth of nature."

This release also can be experienced when we practice meditation and achieve the broader perspective that this life is not everything. Whether or not we recall the experience of diving into the sea of tranquillity during the meditation depends on our capacity for being in touch with our own deepest inner experiences.

Most of the time, we do not remember. We simply experience the pleasant results, and we say, "Meditation seems to work—I don't know how, but it seems to make me feel better."

For Haféz, the bringing of this inner experience of balance and tranquillity to the forefront of daily awareness is the goal of clearheaded and purposeful journeying into intoxication. Relaxing a bit about who and what we are gives us more focus and energy for continuing the pathway of rendi. And as he asserts in the following verse, the rejuvenating road of tranquillity runs in the opposite direction to that of grief, even when we are speaking of death:

> *On my grave don't sit without wine and musician*
> *so that I might wake up from the dead dance.*
>
> *Hold me tight tonight, spirit, although I am old,*
> *so at dawn I wake up young from this trance.*

THE WAY TO BE

Making love, loving life, drinking ruby red wine,
kindred spirits gathered in communion divine.

Cupbearer with sweet lips, a singer of verses,
a partner of pure thought, a trusted friend thine.

A beloved witness clear as life's crystal water,
a seductress of goodness desired by moonshine.

A pleasure house like the palace of Paradise,
a garden therein where health and joy intertwine.

There are guests of goodwill and stewards well-mannered;
friends know the secrets and foes politely resign.

Red wine tart and sharp and so deliciously light,
plums stain love's garnet lips amid tales of the vine.

Cup maiden's long lashes wink like wanton blades;
the curls of that darling cast a net and a line.

A clever entertainer like sweet-tongued Haféz,
a world-wakening teacher who with us does dine.

Reject this rapture and you will live without cheer;
if I don't celebrate, life's spirit is not mine.

Step 14

Giving Way to Abandon

*A*s the rend surrenders to the mystery of the mystical pathway, an inner trust arises in the natural essence of both our visible and invisible environments. We learn to envision the efficiency of nature as the competence of the divine mystery. The next step, then, is learning to trust our inner alchemical change as much as we trust this competent mystery, this rendi.

Haféz was a master in this art of aligning the two worlds, of being in touch with both one's physical being and one's metaphysical double. Working simultaneously from these two frames of reference, he demonstrated firsthand the power of gathered memory. Persian scholars have observed that Khayyam evokes the love of life on Earth while peering into the spirit world; Rumi gives us a whirling, exuberant view of the spirit world itself; and Haféz balances the two worlds. This, again, reflects the concept of biluminosity. And it is also the rapture of life's spirit that Haféz captures in "The Way to Be."

Painting an incredible picture of the most desirable earthly delights united with the highest spiritual qualities, this poem calls up the quality of abandon, a condition that grows out of surrender to competent mystery and opens the heart to further transformation. The first couplet sets the stage:

Making love, loving life, drinking ruby red wine,
kindred spirits gathered in communion divine.

The following verses celebrate the delights of a gathering of friends caught up in the goodness of both world and spirit in a garden "where health and joy intertwine." Even foes, perhaps engaged in the chess matches popular in those times, politely abdicate:

There are guests of goodwill and stewards well-mannered;
friends know the secrets and foes politely resign.

Within this setting, the poet finds his own rightful place, and he invites us all to share this rapture, this abandon:

A clever entertainer like sweet-tongued Haféz,
a world-wakening teacher who with us does dine.

Reject this rapture and you will live without cheer;
if I don't celebrate, life's spirit is not mine.

While abandon opens the heart to the embrace of good friends and a joyous party, it also summons the heart to unite—or rather, reunite—with the beauty and freedom of the natural order. For it was nature itself in the form of the nightingales and roses and lovely surroundings of Shiraz that constantly awakened Haféz:

O smiling flower, inspire the source of my vision
of a full-flowing river that nurtures my taste.

Nature's efficiency is as significant as its beauty. It is the long-term plan and the big-picture vision of every being that conveys the Creator's own enduring energy. While beauty draws our hearts to commune with nature, efficiency makes our minds trust this wild, unknowable, yet completely workable order. In nature, we see the alpha and omega of our own beings, of the seasons, of all life:

Wise bird's nest-building is not meant for forever;
every green spring season seeds brown autumn posthaste.

The opening up of mind and heart to the magnificence of nature's beauty and the precision of its laws creates a sensation of awe and smallness in the human observer. This perception of relative smallness, in turn, threatens the arrogance of the ego, which can burst out and demand instant recognition. This inner reactionary process can take the form of feeling sorry for oneself, of feeling that the ebb and flow of life exist only to wash away one's hopes and dreams.

When this happens, Haféz advises us, create a further opening to the pathway of your imagination by surrendering to your synthesized emotions of awe and mighty resistance. Simply let go of everything, fear nothing, trust that the wonder you witness will sustain you, and accept that even if it doesn't, you have been blessed enough to have experienced the sacred.

Haféz, feel summer passing, now see autumn's wind begin.
It's bittersweet, you understand, each rose must pierce its
    thorn.

In the Company of Like-Hearted Friends

Friends, let us join in waves of beloved's hair;
let its blackness expand this night's joyous air.

Wisdom and unity reign, all friends attend;
close the circle and say a gathering prayer.

Strings of rebec and harp sing out in clear voice;
open your ears to those who speak knowledge rare.

I swear to each friend, you'll be free of grief's veil;
competent mystery's kind if trust it you dare.

No space separates beloved and lover;
if she hesitates, love her all the more fair.

First counsel of Elder has always been clear:
travel not with those ones whose clay you don't share.

If any in circle's not drunk from love's wine,
let's pray for his death while he has life to spare.

If Haféz ever asks for heart-grateful gift,
to beloved's warm lips send him for sweet care.

Step 15

The Blessing of Good Companions

O pening one's life to abandon through surrender creates space into which the rend invites good friends. Some may be friends of the spirit, others of the body, but it is their added presence that brings the final ingredients into the alchemical mixture that fuels the inner process of rendi. Acknowledging these companions and participating with them in creative life processes generate possibilities and pathways that would otherwise remain unknown to us.

Thus far, rendi has directed us to recall ancient ways of making the prayer house shake, to gather our memory toward a goal of truth by focusing awareness on our choice of mythology, to achieve inspiration without fantasy by finding clarity in ecstasy, to develop compassion and generosity by stretching ourselves to embrace the rage of love; and to surrender to the mystery of abandon and the power of competent mystery.

Now comes the sharing of this process with others. The school of alchemy must blend the outside world with its inner universe. Such is the message of "In the Company of Like-Hearted Friends":

Friends, let us join in waves of beloved's hair;
let its blackness extend this night's joyous air.

In this poem of prayer and celebration, Haféz calls up the power of freedom among friends, and he acknowledges the presence of the feminine force of nurturing love throughout all creation:

> *I swear to each friend, you'll be free of grief's veil;*
> *competent mystery's kind if trust it you dare.*

> *No space separates beloved and lover;*
> *if she hesitates, love her all the more fair.*

He also has a word of advice. Rather like the Bible's warning about not casting one's pearls before swine, this verse cautions that it is important to know who your friends are. If you give your faithfulness, it is good to receive the same in return:

> *First counsel of Elder has always been clear:*
> *travel not with those ones whose clay you don't share.*

Throughout his poetry, Haféz stresses the quality of faithfulness as a ruthless, irreversible grounding of one's core in the reality of unity with the sacred. This unconditional honoring of our link to the web of life and the power of creation releases the inner drive for life. When we receive the signals and assistance that we desire from nature in the form of synchronicity, we feel comfortable, loved, and content. However, when things don't go our way, we tend to lose the drive to go on. Haféz expresses this feeling we all know when he says:

> *I am growing old, but not from passing months and years;*
> *it is beloved's unfaithfulness that ages me.*

When doubt arises from a turn of events, the poet brings us this crystal-clear message as an antidote to the weakening of faith:

> *I opt only for patience in your absence,*
> *for patience is the only road I can walk.*

And while you wait in silence and faith, he advises, embrace pain and forget your tears of self-pity arising from the image and feeling of abandonment:

O heart, befriend grief of separation and waiting;
O eye, do not shed any more blood for disunion.

Faithfulness is a steadfast dedication to friendship in the presence
of fantasies and temptations:

Freedom fires the heart that dreams no fear, no greed.
Seduction flirts at every gate to sate our every need.

The blessings of good companionship, then, embody all the
same ups and downs as the rage of love, and one of these turbulent
times is when one must choose between two types of faithfulness.
As the following poem concludes, if you really want to achieve an
expanded mind's broad view of such a situation, it may be better
to stand above it all and look down from the dome of the nymph
of creation as though seeing rivers from a mountaintop.

This poem refers to the Persian tale of the Sheikh of Sanaan,
who abandoned the Islamic religion in order to embrace the faith
of a Christian woman whom he adored. The sheikh found and
expressed faithfulness in deep love for another human and chose
this form of love over adherence to his religious affiliation. This is
a story of connecting with diversity through the singular, unifying
energy of love and finding one's pathway through devoted union
with a beloved companion.

ALL FOR LOVE

Nightingale held the petal so lovely in beak;
but despite this wealth, he sang a song of life bleak.

I asked him, why sigh while you possess such treasure?
He said: Beauty of beloved makes my breath weak.

If beloved walks not with us, I won't protest;
there once was a king who wouldn't mix with the meek.

Our desire and demur move not beloved's heart;
he who senses her essence must forever seek.

Arise, let us admire the brush of that painter
who in her circle with compass etched beauty sleek.

On the path of love don't mourn for reputation;
the great Sheikh of Sanaan pawned his cloak for love's
    cheek.

Libertines enjoy the many pathways of life;
with beads and a cross, the sheikh to angels did speak.

Haféz's vision was molded in dome of that nymph,
as in garden where rivers are seen from a peak.

Profanity Must Go

For quite a long time you have worried me so;
you treat your best friends worse than those you don't know.

Your eyes do not smile in loving approval;
you think the clear-sighted respect such a show?

No flower nor nightingale escapes your grief;
you make us all shout and rend clothes to and fro.

O you who seek heart in the midst of burlesque,
in the profane, the eye of secrets can't glow.

While you are the primrose in garden of sights,
my dear, why ignore me because I am low?

Jewel of Jam's Cup comes from another world's mine;
so why beg for it from the potters' clay dough?

You must empty your bag of silver and gold
to sate desire for silvery beauties and woe.

Intoxication and rendi are my sins;
but without them, says love, my service won't grow.

Haféz, do not spend these good days in complaint;
what do you expect from the passing world's flow?

Step 16

The Realm of Sacredness

*T*he appropriate and effective conduct of daily life is the goal of khater-e majmou—the gathered memory. For Haféz, this means a smiling countenance that conditions the reality around you and converts it into a realm of sacredness. But quite often we are faced with confronting ourselves and others when inner conflicts create outer scowls. Haféz addresses this point early and often in "Profanity Must Go":

> *For quite a long time you have worried me so;*
> *you treat your best friends worse than those you don't know.*
>
> *Your eyes do not smile in loving approval;*
> *you think the clear-sighted respect such a show?*

To perceive this truth and other secrets of life, the rend must get past the basic fantasy of one's own neediness:

> *O you who seek heart in the midst of burlesque;*
> *in the profane, the eye of secrets can't glow.*

The cathartic quality of surrender opens a window to an all-inclusive self-perception that is quite different from the arrogant,

hierarchical perspective of the ego. In humility, preceded by surren-
der, the view and feeling of interconnectedness with the infinite,
interrelated threads of all creatures, vibrations, and sounds fuse
with the force of the ego. Age-old enmity that tends to entangle
itself in one's being disappears. In its place, a mutually enriching
and synergistic partnership emerges. This partnership relaxes the
soul into fearless participation in the flow of life:

> *Intoxication and rendi are my sins;*
> *but without them, says love, my service won't grow.*
>
> *Hafez, do not spend these good days in complaint;*
> *what do you expect from the passing world's flow?*

Achieving the goal of pulling together the gathered memory
involves the acceptance of our smallness relative to the largesse of
the universe, thus making life lighter and pettiness less serious.
Paradoxically, we also realize that the entire universe exists within
our own being or we could not perceive it in the first place.
Given this realization, we no longer seek approval through the
inferiority complex of the ego, but rather we give ourselves with
complete abandon to others, to the world, to the universe at large.
The wine of generosity flows in such a way that the being and the
context within which they exist become indistinguishable. We
become one with the very environment that has nurtured us and
the rest of creation for more than six billion years and that con-
tinuously expands into infinity:

> *Creator, pour rain from the clouds of generosity,*
> *I will become dust and get out of your way.*

The gathered memory is the totality of all your perceptions
about your existence as they assemble in a clear, focused, com-
passionate manner that allows the mind to expand, to embrace
paradox, to love, and to participate with good companions in
the activities of daily life. But this participation must take place
in a sacred, aware manner. Profanity must go. It simply has to
disappear.

Spiritual development, the liberating luster of unity, is not to be sought as a means for fame, material wealth, or a comfort zone in the profane world. Seeking divine unity through partnership with the beloved—the sacred—is an unconditional cry for directly experiencing the magnificent source of all phenomena. You are willing to delve into it despite the uncertainty inherent in the process. You are ready to plunge headfirst:

Such a sacred realm is this pathway of love;
she who arrives is she who loses her mind.

Throw away your books to study in this school,
for the science of love is not in the book.

If you are eager to lose your mind, to spiral into an unknown journey of highs and lows, light and darkness, union and separation, joy and grief, confidence and despair, and to perceive all as equally sacred in the process of self-transformation and connection with the creative source, then:

With the intent of reaching love, take one step forward;
you will gain great treasure as you travel rend's journey.

So it is that Haféz offers guidance for rendi. This pathway of love and its school of alchemy are not about lectures, homework, instructions, exams, counselors, graduation, a profitable job to support your worldly desires, or entry into the ever-fresh Garden of Paradise. If such a vision of benefit from spiritual transformation invades your mind, Haféz once again refreshes your memory with the piercing power of his pen:

The sea of love is not bounded by shores;
there is nothing to do but give your life.

Beware not to reduce freedom, the complete way of the rend, to its tiny parts, the poet cautions. If you become dazzled by new presentations of all-too-familiar spiritual tools and ideas, you will miss the opportunity to directly experience the ecstatic panoramic view of the whole through your own neurological and linguistic senses. In your alchemical process, make sure not to mistake the gleaming rays of the ordinary metals for the unpretentious preciousness of the extraordinary gold. Separating, with utmost subtlety, the gold of your true self from the metals of the false images that inundate your sight is the unparalleled opportunity you experience in the school of alchemy.

That is also when you piece together the school of alchemy's core philosophy as the concept of the gathered memory. Your inner being shifts, and, in turn, the outer may shift as well. Perhaps your own memory of this realization will resemble something like these lines from Haféz:

> *Friend seats me now at the top of the platform,*
> *look at this pauper who now leads this gathering.*

Or this. Imagine the poet looking up at the dome of the mehrab, painted with sky and stars, while lifting his cup of ruby wine in humble salute to wonder and observing simply:

> *Your amorous gesture runs such wine through all lovers*
> *that our reason surrenders and our mind becomes numb.*

EMBRACING ELDER

Your goodness and your charm the whole world does embrace;
O yes, through unity we can conquer world's race.

Candlelight sought secret of our bond to expose;
thank God flame burned its tongue before that sweet disgrace.

Next to this fire that rages in my deepest heart,
the Sun shines as a mere ray to light up sky's face.

Flower wanted to speak of friend's color and scent,
but will of West Wind stills finite words with no trace.

Like needle of compass I once aimlessly roamed
until destiny did my fantasy erase.

The day when the joy of wine cup burned my harvest
was the day cupbearer touched a flame to mind's lace.

Now I want to dance and play in land of Elder,
away from shouts that "end of the world" is apace.

Drink wine, for she who truly sees end of all things
takes up the grape's goblet and casts grief into space.

On rose petal they've etched in blood of our temples
that wise ones have aged like crimson wine in cool place.

Haféz, how can jealousy find fault with your verse
when your poems spring out of the water of grace?

Step 17

The Joy of Imagination

*A*s the traveler on rendi achieves the significant milestone of comprehending the gathered mind, imagination arises as the tool for making best use of this powerful inner resource. From imagination spring creativity, productivity, and joy. In the poem at the beginning of this chapter, Haféz documents the power and potential of spiritual maturity, of seeing beyond one's limited ego. "Embracing Elder" is Haféz's pathway to imagination. He transcends time and space and reaches to the depths of a unified image of humanity through the quintessential Elder, the model of the evolved being we all aspire to become.

> *Your goodness and your charm the whole world does embrace;*
> *O yes, through unity we can conquer world's race.*
>
> *Next to this fire that rages in my deepest heart,*
> *the Sun shines as a mere ray to light up sky's face.*
>
> *Like needle of compass I once aimlessly roamed*
> *until destiny did my fantasy erase.*

The poet remembers clearly his moment of awakening the

gathered memory, and he is fully aware of his own mental surren-
der and its subsequent freedom and abandon. This condition cre-
ates an intense impatience with the self-serving impulse of the
zaheds, who run about shouting that the world is approaching
calamity. Apparently, religious fundamentalists six centuries ago
cried the same warning of the approach of world's end as is being
prophesied today:

> *The day when the joy of wine cup burned my harvest*
> *was the day cupbearer touched a flame to mind's lace.*
>
> *Now I want to dance and play in land of Elder,*
> *away from shouts that "end of the world" is apace.*
>
> *Drink wine, for she who truly sees end of all things*
> *takes up the grape's goblet and casts grief into space.*

Finally, Haféz indulges in a bit of response to his own critics—
the zaheds of Shiraz—by acknowledging the source of his cre-
ativity as the water of grace, another way of linking his own
imagination to the flow of universal mysticism along rendi:

> *Haféz, how can jealousy find fault with your verse*
> *when your poems spring out of the water of grace?*

For Haféz, imagination and joy were parallel qualities. While
Khayyam found joy in the order of the universe and Rumi rev-
eled in the rapture of union with God, Haféz's imagination trans-
lated all phenomena into the beauty of the divine and transformed
everyday occurrences into joyful gifts of the universe. He cel-
ebrated the little explosions of nature:

> *Good news—spring came and buds opened;*
> *my pension on wine and flowers I'll spend.*

> *Wind opens my heart, wine flows free, earth echoes so sweet;*
> *thank you, earth and wine and wind, you taught my heart*
> *   to beat.*

In Shiraz, especially, he saw beauty everywhere. The garden of Mosalla, where he was later buried, became the microcosm of Earth's wonders. The river Roknabad, like Walden Pond for Thoreau, became a mirror for Haféz's own contemplative mind and cleansing tears. Thus, the whole universe became accessible to Haféz through the power of his imagination. This exquisite perspective echoes the evolving process of intelligence that the humanity of the new millennium is moving into: Focus on the smallest parts, see the whole within each of these parts, then act on the entire environment. This is the emerging paradigm of "think locally and act globally" that will permeate social and economic relationships in future decades:

Breeze of Mosalla and water of Roknabad
refuse me permission to travel and sightsee.

Don't fault Shiraz with its Roknabad and pleasing breeze;
Shiraz is the mole on the face of seven nations.

For Haféz, the joy of imagining the whole in the part generates laughter and humor, a natural flow of life that leads to health. He often compares the frowning face of the zahed with the laughing, joyful countenance of dreg-drinkers, and he is not hesitant to express his preference:

While frowning hypocrite sits languishing there,
with open-faced dreg-drinkers I choose to stay.

In this way, the poet sheds his own light on the personality of the zahed, who fears people won't take him seriously or will take advantage of him unless he frowns and puts up a wall. But the beloved, Haféz's pathway to Elder and all-embracing imagination, possesses and values beauty and grace and majesty; she wants to experience Haféz-like laughter, not the frowning face of the zahed. The reason that the face frowns is that it's aware of what it has to hide. If there were nothing to hide, the face could be open to the world and could smile, projecting truth as a mirror of the being's inner condition.

I see no buoyancy of pleasure in anyone,
no heart-healer smiles in dregs of religion.

The joy expressed through laughter and smiling actually can
be seen as the very foundation of the spiritual philosophy of rendi.
The Elder exemplifies this through consistent imageries of hold-
ing up a cup of wine and smiling or laughing before imparting
wisdom. Derived from transcendence, such joy is necessary, the
poet says, for entering the gateway of functionality on Earth. Its
energy brings together disparate beings and spirits into a compat-
ible and coordinated blend of art and science. Haféz sees this blend
as necessary for dissolving the grief associated with the trials of
the world and creating, in its place, the beauty of the future:

Our webbed world's future lies knotted like closed buds;
therefore, float like a spring breeze unfolding new blooms.

I Am Falcon in King's Hands

More than forty years have passed, and still I pretend
to be tiniest servant of my Elder rend.

By the grace of my wine-giving Elder's kindness,
my cup of that purely light wine has reached no end.

In the rank of love and the reign of libertines,
my home is where the throne of tavern does extend.

If I drink the wine's dregs, don't doubt my purity;
my cloak is drunken, but my sober heart does attend.

I am falcon in king's hands; what's come over me
that my source no longer is flight I can intend?

Alas, that nightingale like me lives in this cage;
silent as a lily, my tongue cannot offend.

O how this atmosphere of Fars rears pettiness;
where is companion who does not this place defend?

Haféz, how long would you drink wine under your cloak?
In the vizier's hall, reveal on what you depend.

Let not your reliance on your poetry patron
be like leash forcing proud neck of falcon to bend.

Step 18

Summoning Courage

*D*uring much of our lives, the most significant aspect of walking rendi is overcoming the day-to-day problems that threaten our physical survival and our spiritual and emotional well-being. This goal has been the alchemical purpose of stretching our minds through the examination of paradox. We have become aware of the need to focus awareness, choose a mythology, and seek inspiration without fantasy in order to achieve clarity in personal ecstasy.

In order to maintain well-being, we must understand where this complete process fits within our relationships and choices in the world we share with our companions. We may have imagination, but how do we project it? We may have joy, but how do we protect it? How do we summon the courage to maintain our stance on rendi? One way, Haféz says, is through integrity.

Integrity, to Haféz, is the irreversible oath of freedom—the freedom to choose and express one's pathway of creativity, to long for and to shatter unity, to ease into death. Integrity is independence from the distracting pull of the world, and, as usual in Haféz's philosophy, it embodies an essential paradox. To be truly independent, one may have to enter the door of integrity through dependence. Knowing the elemental truth and being willing to dance gracefully with its intrinsic paradox is the meaning of courage.

In the poem "I Am Falcon in King's Hands," Haféz examines what he considers to be the central conflict and inconsistency of his own life—his dependency on his patron for support. Like artists from time immemorial, he is concerned about "selling out" his true values. But at the same time, he is grateful for the gift of poetry that has filled his life. Obviously composed in his later years, the poem begins by acknowledging the source of his inspiration: the wine, perhaps spiritual, perhaps actual, or more likely some combination of the two forms:

> More than forty years have passed, and still I pretend
> to be tiniest servant of my Elder rend.

> By the grace of my wine-giving Elder's kindness,
> my cup of that purely light wine has reached no end.

But in midpoem, the poet reflects that serving the Elder spirit has been made possible only by also serving his poetry patron. And he worries that this has weakened his tongue:

> I am falcon in king's hands; what's come over me
> that my source no longer is flight I can intend?

> Alas, that nightingale like me lives in this cage;
> silent as a lily, my tongue cannot offend.

He feels alone in Fars, the Persian province where his beautiful Shiraz is located:

> O how this atmosphere of Fars rears pettiness;
> where is companion who does not this place defend?

Finally, the poet sees that direct honesty is the only way to free himself. In one of the few poems that does not end with the last couplet bearing the poet's name, the guiding voice advises him to tell the truth, to identify and acknowledge the patron so that his service to that person does not become a burden. Do whatever you must to survive; this does not mean that you must bow your head in shame:

> *Haféz, how long would you drink wine under your cloak?*
> *In the vizier's hall, reveal on what you depend.*
>
> *Let not your reliance on your poetry patron*
> *be like leash forcing proud neck of falcon to bend.*

In other words, be aware at all times of the two levels of life and their appropriate relationship. Know that the spiritual level of enduring values underlies everything that you do, even though your personal activities sometimes seem to put the deeper level on hold. Perform your daily duties as well as you possibly can while also acknowledging that the transitory nature of existence is bound to erase the results of your work within a relatively short time. Seeing the enduring essence of spirit in relation to the limited span of earthly life enlivens imagination and restores joy.

Haféz's love of life creates hope, which becomes the antidote against the hopelessness that sometimes surfaces when we are faced with odds we know are established but that we have no recollection of having struggled successfully against. Feeling that you can succeed gives you the confidence to go on. It is at this point that Haféz advises us to trust in the ultimate competence of the great mystery of life. You will come to know that your personal road will be paved for you—otherwise you have no desire to go on, even if you find yourself on the road. This becomes important to our future as we face new issues we've not dealt with before. We have to summon this same love of life to go on. Prayer, Haféz advises, is a good way to do this.

Even when you know that destiny watches over you and protects you, the poet cautions time and again, beware of complacency and remember that at any moment things may change for unknown and unknowable reasons. Therefore, pray in order to sustain the effectiveness of your actions. We cannot really control what happens; therefore, it is better to be in tune with natural law through our prayers:

> *We cannot move the Heavens and Earth with our force;*
> *Creator freed the cosmos to run its own course.*

Our prayers strengthen our confidence and summon courage to overcome obstacles. We ask that competent mystery provide well-being, protection, and guidance for that which we seek, need, and value:

> *I pray your body needs no caretaker's caress,*
> *that your delicate soul is not pierced by duress.*

> *The well-being of all worlds depends on your own;*
> *may you live free of pain, no guilt to confess.*

So it is through prayer that we activate our connection between the two worlds that Haféz addresses continually through his poetry's biluminosity. And as that connection brightens with our inner light, we realize that the highest value is to pray first not for our selfish interests but rather for the transcendence of the beloved. For it is the beloved who, in turn, gives us the perspective to transcend our own obstacles:

> *That traveler on one hundred caravans of the heart—*
> *O God, protect her wherever she happens to be.*

Servant of the Soil

I am happy and in loudest voice I say:
I seek West Wind of truth from wine cup today.

While frowning hypocrite sits languishing there,
with open-faced dreg-drinkers I choose to stay.

If Elder doesn't open my tavern door,
where can I go, for whose counsel will I pray?

Do not reproach my rend's spirit in this world;
as I was molded, of that shape is my clay.

See not dervish prayer house nor tavern as path;
God walks as companion wherever I stray.

Dust of rendi is the elixir of joy;
I serve the soil of that ambergris-sweet way.

In the joy of seeing the primrose so high,
by river with cup I stand in tulip's sway.

My story is madness since beloved's curls
tossed me like a ball for her polo club's play.

Bring wine and to Haféz do pray: If heart holds
hypocrites' leftover crumbs, please sweep away.

Step 19

Beyond Mind's Speculations

R emember when you were but an aspiring rend? You were an innocent when you strolled into that tavern in old Shiraz and caught sight of the poet on the corner bench. Remember the seeker asking him about the secret of enlightenment? And his answer was "Focus." That was long ago. Before you trekked step by step along rendi, watching your mind expand as you studied in the school of alchemy. Before you understood that the gathered mind was the aggregate essence of your being in both the material world and the spiritual universe. Before you surrendered to the competence of our life's mystery and its sacred realm.

Now, knowing full well the necessity of joy and prayer-powered courage in facing the paradox of the inner and outer worlds, once again you hear the word "Focus." You blink your eyes. The tavern returns. The poet still sits, sipping from his wine cup. He summons the wine server for another round. The seeker remains, eyes now closed, practicing inner focus. You remember that you entered this tavern long ago, but it seems that no time has passed—or perhaps only a few moments. It seems that something marvelous has happened to you, as though you have realized some cherished dream. You try to consider what has happened, but it is useless. Rather, you hear a short verse:

On love's path there's treasure no one's ever unearthed,
but mind's speculations on its worth are a waste.

Now your eyes go to the eyes of the poet. He smiles and stands, and the room grows quiet. He begins to recite the words he has just scribbled. It is a poem ("Servant of the Soil"), and it is a prayer. His voice is clear and strong and deep:

I am happy and in loudest voice I say:
I seek West Wind of truth from wine cup today.

He acknowledges his choice of fellow rends as valued companions:

While frowning hypocrite sits languishing there,
with open-faced dreg-drinkers I choose to stay.

The ancient Elder is present and his guidance is appreciated deeply:

If Elder doesn't open my tavern door,
where can I go, for whose counsel will I pray?

I am, says the poet, what I am:

Do not reproach my rend's spirit in this world;
as I was molded, of that shape is my clay.

God needs no ceremony or technique on our part in order to appear. Listen for the Creator's presence in all creation:

See not dervish prayer house nor tavern as path;
God walks as companion wherever I stray.

This pathway of sweet intoxication and primroses and tulips—this is the way of joy:

Dust of rendi is the elixir of joy;
I serve the soil of that ambergris-sweet way.

In the joy of seeing the primrose so high,
by river with cup I stand in tulip's sway.

Of course, the entanglements of the outer world make this pathway seem like madness. But while I am bounced about by the world, I know that it is beloved's way of teaching me:

My story is madness since beloved's curls
tossed me like a ball for her polo club's play.

Now the poet opens his arms as though to embrace all in the tavern. As he has offered his poem, so now does he call for more wine—and more purity. His offer to his listeners is the continual awareness of the need to sweep away the ever-clinging crumbs of the hypocrite, both within and without:

Bring wine and to Haféz do pray: If heart holds
hypocrites' leftover crumbs, please sweep away.

The performance has been riveting. You know that you have heard Haféz himself speak. As your mind begins to work again, you realize that this scene has been your school of alchemy for the entire twenty steps of rendi. The poems and guidance of Haféz have come to you as you obeyed the original command: "Focus."

You also realize that your dreamlike vision of this scene has been part of your own gathered memory. And you begin to experience the peace and joy that this understanding brings. Relaxing, you close your eyes. You breathe deeply, and again the voice of the poet sounds. The words are clear. But your inner eyes are open as well. You listen and read in one action. The poem is about our arrival at the goal of truth.

Peace from Despair

As wine seller answers the rends' yearning plight,
Creator absolves sins and puts evil to flight.

Cupbearer, pour wine in chalice of justice,
lest pauper's zeal afflict the world's fright.

Good news of peace can emerge from this despair
if seeker of rendi brings truth to the night.

O sage, if comfort or pain should pass your way,
don't credit the stars—only God grants us light.

In a factory devoid of logic and sense,
will not delusion create fantasy bright?

Musician, now play "no one dies 'til it's time";
those who don't harmonize must then with fate fight.

For me, drained by love and heavy hangover,
only union or pure wine can heal this blight.

Soul melting in wine, Haféz blazing in love,
where is Christ Spirit with its life-giving might?

LET'S DANCE BEAUTIFUL ONE

The breath of West Wind will spray musk in the air;
the old world to its youth again will repair.

Judas tree's agate blooms on jasmine float down;
Narcissus's eye at sweet Adonis does stare.

Hence nightingale's cry of his lonely desire
appeals to the jasmine in her purple tent rare.

Don't blame me for leaving mosque for the tavern;
the sermon was long and time's speed I can't spare.

If today's delight's postponed 'til tomorrow,
who will guarantee the time still will be there?

Keep the cup in your hand all during Shaaban,
for in Ramadan there's no light from Sun's glare.

Flower is precious so value its presence;
when it passes from garden we will be bare.

Musician, ghazals and hymns now let us sing;
stop talk of the past or the future affair.

Haféz to this garden has come for your sake;
so receive him well while time with him you share.

Step 20

Constant Vigilance

*F*or the moment, we must end your visit to the intoxicating nightlife of Shiraz. You are standing on the final step of this exploration of rendi. You may return in meditation any time you wish, but now it is time to take an overview of the steps and lessons. Your studies in the school of alchemy are in recess. Your gathered mind is at peace. You are alert to the goal of truth, the rage of love, the blessing of good companions, and the joy of imagination. Still, you know from the many warnings of Haféz that you must maintain constant vigilance on your process of awareness.

Vigilance is about living in the present and maintaining contact with all of life. With vigilance, you can sustain the strength of inner awareness, the flexibility of mind, and the endurance of emotional stability necessary to live effectively in both your inner and outer worlds. The poem "Let's Dance Beautiful One" paints an extraordinary picture of the power of living in the present. The flow of nature's seasons and cycles is described:

> *The breath of West Wind will spray musk in the air;*
> *the old world to its youth again will repair.*

Judas tree's agate blooms on jasmine float down;
Narcissus' eye at sweet Adonis does stare.

Hence nightingale's cry of his lonely desire
appeals to the jasmine in her purple tent rare.

The poet, in response to the immediacy of life, forsakes the preaching of religion to seek the pleasure of the tavern:

Don't blame me for leaving mosque for the tavern;
the sermon was long and time's speed I can't spare.

If today's delight's postponed 'til tomorrow,
who will guarantee the chance still will be there?

In the Islamic calendar, Shaaban is the month before Ramadan, the month of fasting when wine drinking is forbidden. Haféz advises us to seek, for the time is right. When the flower passes, we will be as bare as the garden:

Keep the cup in your hand all during Shaaban,
for in Ramadan there's no light from Sun's glare.

Flower is precious so value its presence;
when it passes from garden we will be bare.

Again, live in the present. Don't become obsessed with either past or future. And while you're here, by the way, appreciate the poet who's bringing you this message:

Musician, ghazals and hymns now let us sing;
stop talk of the past or the future affair.

Haféz to this garden has come for your sake;
so receive him well while time with him you share.

We live today in an age that is accentuated by the exponential expansion of information. More ideas, facts, and scientific discoveries are being propagated now than ever before and at a rate faster than ever before. To function successfully in this culture, we must practice vigilance in the stretching of our mental and spiritual envelopes. We must absorb facts and arrive at decisions and discoveries through logical deductions. At the same time, we need to appreciate and enhance our inner resources in order to activate the sacred element of guidance that cannot be measured. Therefore, the mind is no longer capable of doing all the calculations. We need to cultivate and train our spirits to join the thinking process. This meeting of mind and spirit inspires both the focus and vigilance aspects of rendi.

To us as readers, Haféz is a voice of love that echoes the sanctity of human intelligence. His poetry reflects the balance between love and intellect, and this balance becomes the source of his genius. This is the same unity that can assist contemporary humanity in cutting through the dizzying effect of the exponential expansion of information in order to find its own heart and soul in a grounded perspective of life. Come, join me, says the poet. After all, you've nothing to lose:

Relent—come, share a cup with me at this table;
it costs you no blood—the grapes have paid already.

As we of the Information Age move into new territories in our thoughts and assumptions, we face the possibility that our current modes of thought may be inadequate in identifying the scope and subtleties of our own potential. The way to move forward at this stage of human thought, Haféz would declare, is the same way that always works. Maintain your integrity through courage, and don't be distracted by the rantings and ravings of the culture at large. This can happen if we learn to project love at all times, while at the same time detaching ourselves from the intensity of the personal desires for approval and control that rest at the base of all human ambition.

As we say good-bye to the tavern of Shiraz and close the door on our personal school of alchemy, we appreciate that our visit has been like a whirlwind tour of the spiraling universe itself. But we also appreciate that the spiritual dimensions of the philosophy of rendi are as applicable to our own present as to the world of

Haféz. Our eyes and ears are key tools that can be opened for us by Haféz for the purpose of surfing the spiritual and physical web of the twenty-first century. All that is required of us is maintaining constant vigilance. As the poet says so well:

This moment starts—arrives—now it is past time;
drink deep, my love, be wise, live this cherished rhyme.

Part 3

In Today's World

The Big Picture

*H*aféz has endured as one of the most inspirational artists in
Persian and world culture because his vision reflects the in-
ner eye of all humanity and his message speaks a truth that rever-
berates within the hearts of awakened people everywhere. His
vision dawns on the spiritual seeker as a stunning realization that
self-transformation is only half the battle. If you feel that the poet
has inspired you toward personal evolution, then another step is
about to appear. You are ready to understand that now it's time to
work on the world. You are part of the whole of humanity, and
your growth has just begun.

Within the context of this vision emerges the message that it
is the feeling for the pulse of all life that brings God. The truth of
Haféz is not some absolute belief system spelling out "right" and
"wrong," just as his pathway is not that of asceticism or renuncia-
tion. Instead, his message is that life opens continuously in front
of our eyes. He advises us to live this directly perceived essence. If
we can't see it, he counsels, drink wine—in whatever form nec-
essary to quicken the spirit and its perception.

For us, as your authors, articulating this range of Haféz's wis-
dom became a matter of decoding his mystic message in terms of

a big-picture vision for humanity at large. This message of unity and expansion is the central thought of virtually all advanced paths of awareness that universal teachers have opened within our collective memory. But Haféz is unique in that his work has retained its stature as spiritual inspiration while it also projects a systematic body of thought and reference points for the social and political fields.

This big-picture application of the wisdom of the poet was the motivation for the 1988 Paris Conference on Haféz, sponsored by UNESCO and attended by scholars from many countries. The purpose for the gathering was to discuss the application of the poet's teachings in the modern world. UNESCO's official statement cited "the great importance of the works of Shams-ud-Din Mohammad Haféz Shirazi and his tremendous influence on Persian literature and on other world literatures and cultures" and "the high esteem in which Haféz is held by countries familiar with the Persian language and literature."[13] Always, however, Haféz remains a consummate artist as well as a universal teacher. His artistry was so esteemed by the popular contemporary poet Forugh Farrokhzad that she called him the only true poet in Iran's premodern literary past, as opposed to other so-called poets whom she considered to be essentially versifiers. This view is shared by other modern Iranian poets as well.[14]

Haféz understood that the mythology folded into his poetry was the story of humanity's journey—past, present, and future. This mythological essence imparted to his work the futuristic quality that renders his vision still relevant. This is what has elicited soaring praise from such spiritual teachers as Inayat Khan and Meher Baba as well as the literary praise of Goethe, Nietzsche, and Emerson. British translator John Payne wrote, "Like Shakespeare, like Socrates, like Mendelssohn, Hafiz was one of the children of the brideschamber who mourn not, for the bridegroom is with them."[15]

Shakespeare, Socrates, and Mendelssohn are just three of the creative geniuses who have demonstrated repeatedly throughout the ages that the leading edge of human thought and inspiration manifests through art. For Haféz, this leading edge can be articulated in his concern for three particular windows through which we can bridge the distance between the world of art and the social and political world of daily existence. These windows, which have become trademark concerns in the serious study of Haféz, are justice, sustainability, and service. They can be defined this way:

- Justice—The most beneficial atmosphere in which to live.
- Sustainability—The visionary focus for our goals, both immediate and long-term.
- Service—The most appropriate personal action through which we can achieve justice and sustainability.

To Haféz, these three qualities exist as art forms, as articulated through his poetry. This means that today's practitioners of these forms are creative artists, and Haféz can be their master teacher. Part 3, "In Today's World," presents his perspectives on these matters.

THE BLESSED REFUGEES

Neither fame nor fortune has called us to this gate;
we approach as refugees, here guided by fate.

We travelers on love's path have journeyed so far
from frontiers of nothingness to this living state.

From Paradise gazing, we saw green on your face
and we came to share growth and to kindness relate.

But guardian Gabriel holds these treasures in trust
so we are now paupers on this kingly estate.

Where's your enduring anchor, O ship of blessings,
why must we drown in guilt while sea's secrets await?

As honor dissolves and parting clouds reveal sin,
hall of justice admits us blacklisted by hate.

Haféz, discard woolen cloak you no longer need,
for first breath warms the soul on this caravan great.

Justice

*P*ersian mythology structures its stories around the eternal war between Ahura, the wise lord of light, and Ahriman, the force of darkness. This war is mediated by the celestial emissary Mithra, the preserver of law and order. Mithra's name originates from *mitra,* the word for "friend" in ancient Sanskrit. His first mythological appearance was as the god Mitra in the Vedas, the sacred hymns of ancient India. Persians consider him both a friend and a protector.

Mithra also represents "contract." He oversees fulfillment of promises and honoring of agreements in all dealings, whether social or business. The symbol of vigilance within every human being, Mithra the mediator watches everything on Earth. He never sleeps; nothing escapes his attention. He holds everyone accountable for what transpires. A practitioner of truthfulness, ethical behavior, and integrity, Mithra does not easily overlook broken promises. If you transgress, he keeps you on the edge of alertness by not telling you for sure what he intends to do—forgive you or throw you into oblivion.

In the renderings of his statues, Mithra often is depicted slaying a bull, an ancient Persian rite that represents the renewal of creation through the passing of light from death into life. This ritual is said to have been instituted by Jamshid, though in most versions of this ancient story he is identified as "Yima," the first human. By slaying the bull, Mithra was believed to renew Jamshid's reign over a world without hunger or death. Contrary to Christian mythology, where the savior—or life force—is sacrificed literally, in the Yima story the *container* of life is sacrificed by purity of attention, as represented by Mithra, in order to allow the life force itself to flow freely again. Ancient Persians believed that the goodness of Ahura ultimately triumphs over the evil of Ahriman.

When Haféz speaks of Jam's Cup, he echoes our yearning for those good times when the inner wakefulness of Mithra served humankind by dispensing justice and sustaining life and civilization. Such good times, Haféz assures us, are what we deserve. Justice is what we want, sustainability is what we need, and service is what we must do. As individual rends, we seek these virtues of justice, sustainability, and service by searching for Jam's Cup. As a collective species, we also yearn for the world-seeing quality of this chalice.

In "The Blessed Refugees," at the beginning of this chapter, Haféz tells humanity's story of coming to Earth in search of these treasures of growth and kindness only to find that "guardian Gabriel holds these treasures in trust." These blessings are not free; rather, all seekers find themselves "paupers on this kingly estate." When they step into the hall of justice so that Mithra can mediate their difficulties on the celestial level, they come face to face with their burden of drowning in guilt:

> *As honor dissolves and parting clouds reveal sin,*
> *hall of justice admits us blacklisted by hate.*

This is our own self-hatred, the poet explains. Our ability to project justice onto the world requires love, the unconditional search for absolute truth, and the capacity to engage in an intimate dialogue with the natural universe within. Born of a single source of creation that is inherently fair, human beings embody the potential to seek and manifest justice. But when the fearful prejudice of good and bad starts overwhelming our psyche and we feel responsible for everything "bad" that happens to us, guilt sets in. The self-hatred embedded in that guilt, Haféz says, tilts the scale against us.

Why not remember, instead of feeling guilty, that we are "travelers on love's path," the intended framework of the universe, and that it was the first breath of creation, the passion for life, that blew us onto this Earth? It is this same breath that ignites the fire of justice within our being. We are one with that which creates us and that which we seek. Because of this unity within all existence, we must give everyone the opportunity to sit in the most prominent position in this world, to rise up to the occasion, and to manifest the highest possible potential. Such a thought inspired this couplet from another poem:

> *On love's path, poor and rich walk just the same;*
> *O king, say the good word with the pauper.*

Justice, Haféz tells us, is empowerment. This principle is rather simple. You recognize within yourself the propensity to do that which is most appropriate, and you activate the natural impulse to act in a way that serves the optimal benefit or highest common denominator of everyone touched by what you do. If you can empower yourself and others with justice, sustainability and service will follow. When you act this way with relative ease, you are in a favorable position to facilitate empowerment in others, so long as that is your intention and their desire.

Because the yearning for justice is a natural substance running through humanity's cells, Haféz says, by denying it we only pour more fuel on guilt's fire. While love of justice can yield great harvests for individuals, communities, societies, and nature as a whole, this same passion can surface as hatred and violence when it is not given the freedom to permeate our lives and keep our inner longing alive:

Cupbearer, pour wine in chalice of justice,
lest pauper's zeal afflicts the world's fright.

Whether caught in material or spiritual poverty, Haféz's pauper, who is robbed of the right to justice because of the arrogance of the king, becomes justifiably angry and hateful. These emotions, in turn, inflame vengeful actions that perpetuate more violent reactions. This cycle of misery, Haféz says from the point of view of someone who sees it all, can be broken only with justice. This is the truth into which we must tune. This is the dream we must bring into being:

O king of goodness, ride with your bridle in check;
no stop on the road lacks a claimant of justice.

Throughout Haféz's teachings, one reality stands out: The way we treat another creature always returns to affect our own well-being:

Listen to the old farmer's sweet words to his son:
Apple of my eye, you'll reap no more than you sow.

This, of course, is Haféz's restatement of the Christian proverb of virtually the same wording, the Sanskrit principle of karma, and a homily that has been repeated endlessly throughout the world's wisdom teachings. But let us take the thought one step further and ask the poet: What is it exactly that we, the humanity of the twenty-first century, must sow?

Plato's "essential knowledge," Haféz might well respond. Like the Persian philosopher Avicenna centuries earlier, Haféz knew and loved the works of Plato:

Who else can reveal essential knowledge to us
but Plato, that finely aged wine in a barrel?

When Haféz talks with passion and abandon about justice, he echoes the clear-sightedness that emanates from what Plato termed "essential knowledge," a concept that was well within Haféz's grasp as a master of philosophy and mathematics. Essential knowledge is the awareness and deep understanding of the laws that govern creation—the laws through which the mind gains its insights and capacity for comprehension. It provides the seeker of truth with tools for mastering the science of mediation in the search for justice. The single mean that binds the extremes of a given dilemma is the balance sought by the practitioner of justice.

The kindness of justice is also addressed in these lines of Haféz, said to be inspired by Plato's "forms," which the Greek philosopher theorized that we saw before our birth and therefore remember and seek to find again:

Beauty and loving existed before either world;
image of kindness was not sketched in this time alone.

As the vivid imagery of Haféz's poetry helps us envision, justice is the heart of all creation. It is a profound feeling of oneness with all else in the universe. Far from being a ship of emotions rocked by our reactions to the turbulent sea of outside stimuli, the feeling of justice has its home in the heart's ocean of tranquility. Within a trustworthy expanse of deep silence, anchored by the non-prejudicial condition of biluminosity, the seeker of truth gains access to the vibrations of justice through the perception and embodiment of unity in existence at large.

In Western culture, this unsurpassed capacity for balanced mediation and judgment is represented by the image of justice as a blindfolded woman holding a scale on which evidence is weighed. She stands in deep reflection, her eyes shut to the outside world. Appearances don't affect her. She is oblivious to whatever outer eyes tend to see: the color of skin, clothing, adornments, elements of face and body, height, weight, physical condition. In many images, the blindfold covers the justice's ears as well as eyes, rendering her nonreactive to any outer communication.

Another Haféz couplet said to reflect his study of Plato also speaks of the eye of inner seeing:

To see your beauty requires eyes of deep vision;
how can my own poor eyes perform such a great task?

Blind and deaf, justice is immune to the distracting pull of myriad forms and multiple voices. Always starting from a foundation of blankness, at the clear-sighted point of zero, the justice-seeking feminine force focuses her entire attention on perceiving and hearing with inner eyes and inner ears. She experiences biluminosity, the double enlightenment of inner balance and suspended judgment. She looks inward to find the appropriate answer, and what she retrieves from her inner hall of justice influences the movement of the scale she holds.

In another, less familiar version of the statue of justice, the woman is not blindfolded. She simply looks away from the scale so that her decision is not necessarily determined by how the weights fall in the short term. Instead, her stance embraces a projected vision in search of long-term considerations. The essence of justice involves her ability to summon the inner vision not only to do the right thing in the present but also to awaken the wisdom to understand how her immediate decisions may affect the future and facilitate an appropriate balance in the long run.

Such an enormous feat is a demonstration of the genius of the heart and the meaning of justice. It is the quality of an appellate judge—someone with an expansive vision, intimate knowledge of precedents, unshakable integrity, and a deep desire to succeed where other judges have failed. Haféz's appellate judge is Pir-e-Moghan, the Elder who can see far and wide and can gauge not only the short-term results of a particular decision but also its long-term implications for humanity's evolution. In still another couplet attributed to the poet's musings on Plato's theory of forms, the imagery of the domed prayer house of Pir-e-Moghan is invoked:

> Before this green ceiling and this azure dome were built,
> the brows of beloved arched a roof over my eyes.

Within the dream of justice, Haféz warns us through his Elder, we must accept the mystery of polarized duality within unity, and, instead of trying to understand the unknowable, we must immerse our souls in the very heartbeat of the universe and the wine of love and awareness. For Haféz, this is the function of poetry. Perhaps someday, he sings in many verses, we may come closer to the answer.

Universal mysticism and Plato's essential knowledge also state that it is the law of creation that elements are fulfilled through their opposites. With the biluminous feeling of impartiality, justice seeks the midpoint between extremes, the distance between the black of the white and the white of the black. While balance is the unifying intersection of opposites, it is far from being diluted truth. In fact, unity cannot be perceived as being divided into two equal parts, because with equality there is no difference, and without difference there is no perceptual universe.

Justice, therefore, may emerge through either vice or virtue, since both contain the seed of truth. Both are illumined—each in a different way, for a different purpose. Who is to say that going up is better than coming down, Haféz asks. And in the same breath, he gives his answer:

> *As to faithfulness, you are not reliable,*
> *but I thank God that you stand against tyranny.*

Haféz assures us, from the point of view of a spiritual master and a poet who survived while speaking the truth during highly violent times, that the breath of creation is free from the malice of oppression. The universe is a series of checks and balances destined to create the freedom of suspended judgment—the very balance we also seek. Nature works in such a way that elements reach the mid-point in the long run even if there are disasters—appearances of injustice—in the short term. To wash away the clouds of bias about high and low, just observe the workings of nature. A blooming tulip that we call beautiful is in no way superior to a crawling insect:

> *Friendship with dervishes can accompany greatness;*
> *in all his grandeur, Solomon was a friend of ants.*

Haféz also distinguishes between justice and revenge. One is a universal concept with its eye on a long-term balance. The other is merely a short-term payback. With the gentleness of a caring friend who wants to take our minds off banality for a moment and infuse confidence by helping us remember that we are bonded with life through a more expansive universe, the poet encourages qualities such as forgiveness and mercy:

In book I seek guidance to better know ethics:
faithfulness and mercy, virtues of the divine.

Enemy who oppresses you to immense pain—
give riches to him like a generous gold mine.

Be no less giving than the sheltering shade tree,
the one who throws stones at you, do feed him fruit fine.

Learn from oyster the subtle art of forbearance;
she yields precious pearl to those who on her flesh dine.

The virtues of forgiveness and mercy also anchor our desire to sustain humanity's existence and its quality of being. It is easy to imagine that if Haféz were among us today, he would smile with the wondrous eyes of a child and with the abandon of a being who is fully trusting of what is. Look at your world, he might suggest, look at the delicate balance between the globe's male and female populations: 49.5 percent men and 50.5 percent women, enough to tip the scale toward the qualities that we need to nurture at this moment in history, but not such an edge as to create a comfort zone that would produce complacency and stunt our yearning to stretch and reach out to our opposites. This is the wake-up call of nature, the workings of a universe that we humans have helped to shape and which, in turn, keeps us on the cutting edge of our consciousness. This way, we may remember that progress happens when we manage successfully to walk the tightrope of duality.

Another possibility for manifesting humanity's search for justice, Haféz might point out, is the field of potential partnership between the nations of the Northern and Southern Hemispheres. The two halves of the globe have been segregated along the lines of "developed" and "underdeveloped" countries, caught in the stagnation of slavery and sultancy. Do we have the courage to imagine the reality that might result from the alchemy of the best of both worlds' perspectives, knowledge, and resources? As the poet would ask, are we willing to rid ourselves of the toxic potion of guilt, neediness, and condemnation, and allow golden ingenuity to fill the cup of our collective spirits? Are we ready to grasp the simple truth that the basic human right is the right to feel whole and see clearly? Then again, Haféz would laugh with his cup of wine raised to our potential; our quest for human freedom and our yearning for the marriage of North and South are a reflection of the love exchange we seek between our bodies and souls, between Heaven and Earth. Justice is a state of mind and heart, and we will reap on the outside that which we sow within.

In order to manifest this crop of justice, we must ask ourselves what price we are willing to pay for it. For one thing, we must abandon our arrogance, Haféz says. We need to destroy the hierarchical mind-sets of ourselves and of our cultures as well as the structures and systems that replicate those mind-sets. Any sense of superiority is obsolete within the reality of interconnectedness:

> *Flower is beloved, bless your communion together;*
> *like yours, her pathway to and from the garden is sacred.*

But the sacrifice that we make must be an act of cleansing and release, leading to liberation, like the rejuvenating sacrifice of the bull to Mithra the mediator. In other words, the sacrifice is to be an act of service. We must understand that we are all part of the divine unity and that our actions serve that unity:

> *Every human and angel is love's parasite;*
> *Jam's Cup bestows nothing on those lacking clear sight.*

As humanity travels on in time and space, as we evaluate our stance on justice, and as we work through the complexity of our hierarchical systems and structures, Hafez's timeless wisdom gives us a model of evolution through which our consciousness stretches so much that we can feel and embrace the magnificence of our original unity. This wisdom challenges us to grasp the reality of duality and respond to contradictory events with a potent combination of intuition, reason, and rapture, a universally intended balance that we have the right to master.

The application of justice requires intellectual competence, undivided focus, and the globe-seeing heart of the rend. You must be fully aware of precisely who is in front of you, what that person represents, what you must learn from the situation, what act to perform that would bring about your mutual freedom, and how to accomplish the task in a way that generates long-term benefit for everyone affected.

This is a tall order. But, as Hafez insists, anything short of such integrity is only lip service to justice. The quest for unabated truth is humanity's irreversible mission. This is a journey of individual and global transformation that we must travel with courage, joy, and purposefulness in order to create a critical mass capable of tipping the scale of events to the side of justice. This is our gateway to infinite freedom and progress. On this caravan, we have everything we need. We have poetry to inspire and liberate our souls, and we have the wine of unity to intoxicate our minds, inflame our passion, and keep our yearning alive.

And, on this journey, should we come face to face with antagonistic forces, Hafez smiles knowingly, let's consider them as allies. Enemies are merely the flip sides of friends; they both come from the same atom. Hafez's poems continually echo the essential reality that from a single source of creation emerge mutually repellent forces in a state of separation. This is how life is formed and how the fire of relationship is ignited. Hafez, the justice-seeking rend, owes his own growth and liberation to the presence of his enemy, the zahed, the highly judgmental, fundamentalist practitioner of piety and hypocrisy.

The *mohtasseb* is the establishment's "sheriff," the enforcer of the law who also gives himself permission to make his own rules as he arrests people for such sins as drinking wine or chanting about oneness with God. But behind the veil of puritanism, the mohtasseb himself drinks wine; he longs for spiritual freedom. To Haféz the rend, at war with false righteousness and self-denial, the nature of justice is such that even the sheriff's hypocrisy merits praise, for it contains hidden lessons in the search for balance:

O heart, learn the way of rendi from mohtasseb;
although he is drunk, no one ever suspects him.

In the same breath of an all-embracing spirit, Haféz also sends this generous message to the spiteful king of his time:

The king will gain more from one hour of justice
than from one hundred years of worship and prayer.

By putting such tolerance and compassion on our plate of alternatives to fundamentalism and one-sidedness, Haféz invites us to realize that we can become one with another creature's heartbeat when we allow ourselves to draw close, listen, and observe subtleties with an eye keenly searching for binding threads. Perhaps we will even embody the sensations that others experience.

However, after such immersion, the poet also warns us, distance yourself in order to focus on the spectrum, to observe how each part stands alone in its distinct beauty with its inherent cycle of life and death. See how all parts of creation, so different in their colors and forms, relate to one another in a beautiful symphony of beginning and ending.

In such moments, Haféz whispers to us, do not strain to understand the mystery of splitting diversity, of being and nothingness. Instead, continue to listen for the song of togetherness by sharing poems, beauty, and wine with those you once considered your enemies. Allow your empowered visions of justice to expand to their full limits; the answer you seek will come in due time.

MAKING PEACE WITH ENEMY

With regal bearing walked king of sweet lips today,
he whose gaze through lashes his enemy does slay.

While drunkards passed by me and saw just a pauper,
O you, igniter of sweet tongues, the king did say.

Your pouch is barren, I see, of silver and gold;
come join my silvery beauties, take servant's pay.

You're no less than light particles, rise, seek the Sun;
whirl with body and soul and at source you will play.

Don't lean on this world while the wine cup you embrace;
take joy from wide Venus brows and forms that do sway.

My wine-drinking Elder whose spirit I salute
advised me from the road of trust-breakers to stray.

Embrace all as your friend and forgive every foe;
be servant to God and wave the Devil away.

At dawn midst red tulips the West Wind I addressed:
All these bloody shrouds—for whom did these martyrs pay?

O Haféz, said Wind, this is beyond you and me;
instead, let's talk poets and wine's ruby bouquet.

Riders, Where Are Thee?

I see no trust among people; friends, where are thee?
When did companionship end? Lovers, where are thee?

Water of life is soiled; has soul of Khezr vanished?
Blood pours from flower stems; breeze of spring, where are thee?

No one says a friend merits friendship in return.
Truth-knowers, what happened? Companions, where are thee?

No ruby for years from mine of humanity.
What's become of sunshine? Wind and rain, where are thee?

This was a land of good friends and compassion.
When did our kindness disappear? Kings, where are thee?

The polo ball of greatness waits at center field;
no players come to the horses. Riders, where are thee?

Hundreds of thousands of flowers bloom, no bird sings.
Nightingales, why hushed? Thousand-strong flock, where are thee?

Aphrodite's music stopped as though her lute burnt.
No one aspires to freedom. O rends, where are thee?

Haféz, no one knows divine secrets, seek silence.
Don't ask just anyone: Wheel of time, where are thee?

Sustainability

F or Haféz, the act of sustaining passion for life and kindness through evoking the spirit and practice of love starts by recalling the beloved. In Sufi mysticism as well as in the more ancient traditions echoed in the poet's imagery, the beloved is the representation of the feminine essence, the most evolved form of divine beauty on Earth:

> *Although I have grown old and tired and weak,*
> *my youth returns when I recall your face.*

Through the symbolic understanding of the feminine, we engage in spiritual transformation, a necessary process for sustainability. During painful times, when doubt invaded his psyche and the pain of separation tore his heart, Haféz evoked the image of the beloved just as today's "modern pagan" movement recalls the inspirational qualities of the Neolithic goddess. Like the poet, people still reach out for an essential core that is undeniably a part of us, one that has been lost for a long time:

> *The mist of hair clouds her sunlike face, O God,*
> *may she sustain as eternally as her goodness.*

In this context, Haféz's sustainability is the capacity to maintain the thread of a vision and its corresponding manifestations long enough to create results that continue to inspire even when the catalysts of the original vision are removed. Such capacity retains the enduring relevance of old principles while reorganizing it into forms that serve the changing needs of society.

This type of sustainability is at the heart of the evolutionary process. Its challenge always has preoccupied humanity during critical junctures of growth. Today, as we stand at our modern crossroads of technological hope and its potentially alienating despair, we need to awaken a deep level of wisdom that will help us make appropriate decisions. Our choices will determine not only how we live in the short term but also how succeeding generations will live in the distant future. This deep and unconditional caring for what is yet to come—that which we may not live to witness—is the love of life embedded in sustainability.

When embroiled in a painful situation of injustice, violence, or greed, in order to rekindle the passion necessary to sustain his vision of peace, Haféz remembered the best of the world's past. He recalled with pride the voices of egalitarian philosophies and the spirit of community that once reigned in his land. "Riders, Where Are Thee?"—the poem at the start of this chapter—is an example of Haféz's antidote for grief and despair. The following couplet, one of the most vivid products of his creative visioning, is a verse often quoted by contemporary Iranians:

> *The polo ball of greatness waits at center field;*
> *no players come to the horses. Riders, where are thee?*

This is Haféz's invitation to remember and then harness the natural instinct for justice and cooperative prosperity that once ran like wild horses within our hearts before our collective psyche was numbed by the decaying weight of civilization.

An earlier line of the same poem asks:

> *Water of life is soiled; has soul of Khezr vanished?*

This question captures the essence of sustainability. The Persian mythological figure Khezr corresponds to the Old Testament prophet Elijah. Various Christian interpretations of the New Testament claim that Elijah was reincarnated as either John the Baptist or Jesus. In other mythologies, Khezr's spirit is likened to the angel Gabriel's. The Middle Eastern myth, as told in the Koran, is that Khezr reached immortality by finding and drinking the water of life (the "fountain of youth" in Persian literary texts). According to this story, the water of life resides in "the gloom" or "land of darkness."

The fountain of youth is the clarity of vision that emerges from purposeful immersion in difficult times and thereafter endures through time and space. In the many versions of the myth, Khezr—or Elijah—endured many trials in order to journey from his status as an ordinary man to a learned being of extraordinary knowledge with a capacity for miracles and a penchant for prophecy. He thus gained the wisdom to counsel kings and is reported to have guided Alexander the Great to the fountain of youth. However, Alexander, with all his material might and military victories, could not find the water of immortality, because, as Haféz puts it:

The water of life flowed not to Alexander,
for this gift is not won by force and riches.

Khezr's name also signifies "green"; the story is that wherever he walked and put his feet, greenery covered the earth. This image of green—which in modern humanity's psyche summons the vision of environmental protection and ecological health—weaves with the nurturance of soul to provide an inner strength to surmount hardships and gain strength through integrity, resourcefulness, and patience.

However, at times, Haféz says, even the clarity of Khezr's soul can become soiled when violence and alienation proliferate and we become vulnerable to losing our original purpose and direction of unity. Again, from "Riders, Where Are Thee?":

This was a land of good friends and compassion.
When did our kindness disappear? Kings, where are thee?

During murky times, when vision is blurred, Haféz encour-
ages us to call on "the breeze of spring"—a fresh perspective that
is rooted in awakening a yearning for the best of the past. This is
because the higher states of consciousness and humanity we strive
for already exist in our experience, at least as Plato's phenomenal
forms if not as absolute states of being. Therefore, our consider-
ation of sustainability is not only a view of humanity's forward
motion but also a remembrance of our collective past and the
accumulated knowledge of the human species that can inform
our actions. This is the principle of gnomonic or cumulative
growth. In Haféz's poetry, this idea often comes through the im-
agery of the seashell, in which the traces of the previous stages of
growth carry over and become clearly discernible in subsequent
stages. The following couplet is another observation of the same
principle:

Recalling your eye, I build the ancient prayer house
where we will resurrect the structure of the old pact.

But Hafez's "old pact" is not a regression into obsolete pat-
terns. Rather, it is a recapturing of the values that have persisted
through humanity's evolution and suggest the eternal quality that
we term "immortality." In other words, two thousand years from
now, the ultimate goals of our personal quests may be the same as
today, although our questions undoubtedly will change and our
entry points into the inquiry and the tools we employ in the search
may vary considerably.

The thread that sustains the vision of unity and prosperity
through the darkest times in human evolution, including during
Haféz's own life, is, quite simply, reverence for life—love. Here is
a famous couplet recited regularly by spirited Iranians as a re-
minder of this simple truth:

The heart enlivened with love will never die;
our endurance is inscripted in life's journal.

Love of life, Haféz says, naturally breeds kindness of heart within oneself and toward the rest of creation. It weaves the carpet of humanity with unbreakable threads that carry forth our imagination of connectedness and collective prosperity through time and space.

> *Every building you see is destructible*
> *except the enduring shelter of kindness.*

Human beings have the capacity to stretch indefinitely by expanding their consciousness. Such an act is not out of the realm of possibility according to theories of consciousness studies and quantum mechanics, though it may be quite unsettling to minds that view humanity within only a limited material framework.

One of the most eloquent articulations of this infinite possibility of growing and stretching remains that of George Bernard Shaw, who wrote with his typical humor that Haféz undoubtedly would have enjoyed:

> We have to face the fact that we are a very poor lot. Yet we must be the best God can as yet do, else He would have done something better. I think there's a great deal in that old pious remark about us all being worms. Modern science shows that life began in a small, feeble, curious sort of way as a speck of protoplasm that, owing to some willingness, some curious striving power always making for higher organisms, gradually that little thing constantly trying, wanting, having the purpose in itself, being itself a product of that purpose, has, by mere force of wanting and striving to be something higher, gradually, curiously, miraculously, continually evolved a series of beings, each of which evolved something higher than itself. What is to be the end of this? There need be no end. There is no reason why the process should stop since it has proceeded so far. But it must achieve, on its infinite way, the production of some being, some person if you like, strong and wise, with a mind capable of comprehending the whole universe and with powers capable of executing its entire will. In other words, an omnipotent and benevolent God.[16]

In terms of universal mysticism, this very transformation of human beings into a mirror of their Creator is the precise intent and goal of evolutionary unity. We get glimpses of this destination during ecstatic raptures brought about through vision quests, meditation, sexuality, or emotional bonding with others. At such times, sustainability manifests as the capacity to prolong experiences of union with our creative source to the point of a critical mass that transforms banality into a new reality where the sacred enters and thrives. This is the law of manifestation as explained in the Hermetic epistemology that runs through Haféz's poetry. This is what twentieth-century theoretical scientists term "whole systems thinking." This is the goal of the creative process.

Any process of creation—the unveiling of the sacred in human experience—originates from a full embrace of the archetypes in the universe of potentiality. These archetypes represent the possibilities contained within the absolute, in some traditions referred to as the divine qualities or divine names. The creative act of accessing the forms of divine primordial spirit, directly perceiving their movements and meanings, and bringing them forth into material forms reachable by ordinary senses is what we call art.

The vehicle of art may be painting, poetry, creative writing, music, dance, performance, partnership, leadership, or service to others. The purpose of art is to manifest in concrete and palpable terms the abstract phenomena that capture our imagination and enhance our yearning to experience those phenomena through our bodies and as an extension of our human forms.

Keeping the drive alive long enough to actually materialize our visions of the sacred is the art and science of sustainability. It is art because it demands direct connection and participation in the spirit world. It is science because it requires deep inquiry, meticulous observation and processing of what we learn, and continuous expansion of the intellect to strengthen the periphery of our vision to inquire into more penetrating questions.

But, as Haféz demands in his ingenious blending of art and science, we must be thoroughly patient while engaged in the creative process. In fact, sustainability is synonymous with endurance. It is also a friend of victory:

> *Patience and triumph are old good friends;*
> *because of patience comes triumph's turn.*

And again:

> *Palate of my heart did not reach your lip;*
> *she said: Wait, and your wish will be granted.*

When our tendency is to fail and fall back on the destructive practices and thought forms that we are striving to transform, Haféz jolts us into keeping our focus on the truth of union. Go for the absolute, he encourages us, instead of symbols:

> *Tomorrow when the house of truth does arise,*
> *traveler in allegory will feel lost there.*

> *O graceful partridge, where are you going—stop;*
> *be not misled by pious cat in prayer.*

The tale of Haféz's personal development in his youth demonstrates the power of perseverance and focus on the whole vision rather than on incomplete images. This story, an extension of the poet's affinity with the prophet Khezr, tells of his love for a beautiful woman named Shakh-e-Nabat. Fully taken with the breathtaking grace of this young maiden, Haféz commits himself to seeking Khezr's spiritual guidance in finding the source of poetic inspiration in order to express his love. Determined and fearless, the poet embarks on a forty-night vision quest in a spot called Pir-e-Sabz (the Green Old Man) outside Shiraz, his hometown. For thirty-nine days, every morning he walks by Shakh-e-Nabat's window in order to intensify his desire, and at night he sits vigil accompanied by the terror-provoking apparition of a fierce lion.

On the fortieth morning, the maiden announces her readiness to marry Haféz, this penniless poet whom she deems preferable to a wealthy prince. But Haféz decides to finish his fortieth-night vigil. On that last night, an old man dressed in green appears in his vision, brings him the water of life, and gives the young man the golden pen of poetry. Filled with the ecstasy of his fulfilled wish, Haféz realizes that his true desire is poetry itself, the gateway to freeing his soul, and not Shakh-e-Nabat. True, an image of beauty compelled him to embark on a search of his deepest self. But ultimately it was only the source itself, the elixir of love, that had the power to quench the poet's thirst.

To dissolve the seeds of doubt and complacency, Haféz says, maintain the intoxication of undivided passion and act within it— and do it today:

Value this garden and drink wine today,
for next week, the flower will not exist.

Remember too that it is fantasy to insist that anything necessarily exist forever. Insisting on that idea may convert the desire for sustaining the highest potential of life into arrogant self-assertion— fundamentalist drives intended to establish the immortality of one's ego through name, reputation, wealth, or offspring. Everything exists only to fulfill its inherent purpose as guided by and aligned with the natural order of phenomena. If forms existed forever, life as we know it would not endure. Life needs change—the death of one form and birth of another—in order to thrive. Without duality and difference there would be no growth.

For this reason, Haféz says, understand and accept the wisdom of darkness, the cleansing quality of shadow. The poet himself lived during one of the darkest times in Iran's history. He was born in a neighborhood of violent gangs and spiritual charlatans. Perhaps it was this very contradiction that offered Haféz the opportunity to thrive in art, grow in science, and leave behind a body of work with a depth of perception and enduring relevance that have captured the imagination of thinkers throughout the world.

From Haféz's own poetry we learn that creativity requires entering wakefully and surrendering fully to a dichotomous situation. It calls for embracing or plunging into the world of shadows, which are both hostile forces as well as the tools of our freedom. Even though they are seemingly repulsive, shadows are in reality our allies, simply because they exist within the space from which our potential for creativity emerges. They may show up as fear, grief, a person who "pushes our buttons," or other forms and vibrations that evoke resistance and encourage combative reactions to the creative process.

Shadows appear as the barriers that hold us back and prevent us from moving forward with passion, purpose, clarity, and ease. Hopelessness, despair, and all other forms of disempowerment call up and project the shadows. They kill our initiative, shatter our sense of authentic self, pillage our constructive ideas, and prevent us from seeking the deeper meanings of life. Shadows are highly skilled shape-shifters that demand utmost vigilance on our part. But regardless of what form they take, one definite characteristic of shadows is that the more and harder we fight them, the more strongly they fight back.

That is why, as in Haféz's biluminosity, the means of our transformation often resides in our entering the darkness and becoming one with it. This, however, requires understanding that the purpose of the shadow is to cast light on the source to whatever degree we, as human observers, have developed the capacity to persevere and derive meaning from it. It also necessitates the realization that the disorienting dark forces of chaos, contradiction, and doubt contain within them excellent opportunities for learning, developing new skills, and mastering the shadow's art of shape-shifting fluidity.

The dance of light and darkness is a mystery, Haféz reminds us again and again. Although we must always stay focused on our search and stretch our imaginations into inconceivable territories, we also must trust that the reason the divine world veils its light with a shadow is that the light of the source otherwise would be too blinding. Even the ecstasy of Khezr's fountain of youth pales relative to the wholeness of creation:

As the water of life touches friend's lip,
it becomes clear Khezr saw only a mirage.

In Persian mythology, shadows are symbolized by dragons. They represent the place of encounter between the Moon and the Sun, the feminine and the masculine, within. If we resist the opening of our Moon (the mystic's heart), we run the probable danger of losing our heart (our intuitive power and sensibilities) altogether. But if, in full consciousness of the perils and with complete awareness of our intent and timing, we temporarily align ourselves with the dragon, the animal metamorphoses from a soul-devouring beast into a nurturing container of conception.

Haféz's poetry is a constant reminder that the darkest time is the hour before dawn. From the bottom of paralyzing despair also can come the fiery impulse to reach our destination. The pre-dawn imagery in Haféz's poetic rhythms portrays wise beings, angels, and beauties of all types appearing in the poet's dreams and helping him awaken from the black fog of aimlessness to the blissful brightness of self-actualization:

Just before dawn, awakened destiny appeared
and said: Arise, beloved's lover has arrived.

Take your cup and gracefully walk toward the scene
to see the splendor that your vision has contrived.

In the same breath, Haféz also echoes with equal lucidity the importance of not dwelling too long in the shadow and the numbness of its extreme form of apathy. Use your time with the dragon as a cathartic experience, he says, not as a magnet for addiction to the life-sapping energy of grief. Pass by the shadows quickly, before depression becomes a norm and your journey is unnecessarily delayed. The best tool for this crucial and time-bound transition from grief to joy, an important skill in sustainability, is confidence—a constant return to the center of your self. You fully remember the flow of life and forget all else instantaneously. This, again, is the concept of khater-e majmou, the gathered memory.

As you reach and enhance your wholistic mind through expanded imagination, the capacity for perceiving meaning increases. In balancing this depth of perception with common sense (the ability to see the forms of things) and practical knowledge of how things work, you are able to make manifest in reality the divine qualities to which you aspire. To those of us with a passion for creating and sustaining a vision in measurable form, Haféz says:

> *The sunlike wine rose in the East of the chalice;*
> *if you seek the leaf of pleasure, arise from sleep.*

Given his own mystical and worldly experiences, Haféz would empathize deeply with those of us facing profound extremes in a new epoch in human history, this age of unparalleled potential for creative change and fulfillment intertwined with unprecedented violence and alienation. He reminds us that the human form is the place for gathering the separate dualities of the inner and outer. In the many wars we wage among nations and people grow the very seeds of peace. Within the increasing gap between rich and poor peoples rest opportunities for creating intentionally balanced and egalitarian communities. From our deepening addiction to computers springs a deep passion for connecting with kindred spirits and experiencing the freeing power of the human touch.

If we ask Haféz to comment about our dream of a techno-paradise creating more leisure and an easier life for all, about its promise of increasing the spirit and practice of altruism, and about its vision of empowering children to lead freer lives, he will speak with us humorously, yet firmly:

> *Set piety's cloak afire, let curve of cupbearer's brow*
> *pierce the dome atop the spot where the imam preaches.*

This is Haféz's way of saying, "Don't sell me the shortcuts of your paradise of technology—what I need will appear; beauty of nature is my window to expanded imagination. Tell me, do you have the courage to lose your mind to the beat of love?" The poet tells us with his usual biluminous alertness to the constantly praying, false, pious zahed—or imam (Shiite Moslem religious leader)—that the paradise we seek is in the spontaneous grace of those who bring our feelings to the brim of expression. It is the act of fully engaging in the transformation of reality every moment of our existence rather than in the promise of a better future. Burn with the passion of balance, Haféz whispers, keep your feet on the ground. Everything will come in due time, but you must learn the art of tempering contradictory elements. This is the art of negotiation:

> *My heart accepted chaos from the loop of her hair;*
> *I will never know what profit it saw in this deal.*

Sometimes we have to let go of instant gratification in order to achieve something of more profound value with farther-reaching consequences. As we enter the new millennium, mutually empowering negotiations between people and the fusing of material success with effective application of cooperation and stewardship become our training grounds for spiritual transformation. As we hold our focus on this field of growth, as we build concrete examples of empowering performance in education, business, families, and communities, we establish a body of knowledge and inspiring stories that can both sustain our own drives and fuel the creative visions of coming generations.

As in "Riders, Where Are Thee?," by intensifying our inner yearning for the constructive and liberating realities we desire and by gathering together those who share our passion, we create the foundation of a collective dream that is compelling enough to capture the imagination and engage the participation of future generations. This is sustainability in action. As we continue our efforts in the direction of a more balanced world, Haféz stands with us as a friend and also as an elder if we choose to seek his guidance. The poet addresses these words to the youth of our times:

> *Listen to counsel, O dear one, for prospering youths*
> *cherish more than life the guidance of a learned elder.*

The alignment of elder and youth is a recurring theme in Hafez's poetry. The elder ("elder" here can refer to an older person, not just Pir-e-Moghan) is not a fundamentalist teacher or preacher, but more likely a storyteller—someone who shares illuminating life experiences and enduring wisdom with the younger generation. To Hafez, the affinity between elder and youth is an engine of sustainability, a thread that connects the primordial flash of life and lessons of the past to the benefit of the future. Such bonding, the poet says, is the mirror image of life itself:

If you desire that beloved not break your pact,
hold tight to the thread so that she will do the same.

For strengthening our connection with the web of creation, Hafez prescribes all forms of perceiving, absorbing, and projecting beauty. This beauty we can see everywhere and in everything—in the face of a child, in the dance of dervishes, in the tired hands of a farmer, in the ease with which friends converse.

Once again, relating to and expressing beauty is the essence of art. The material in the beauty observed by the perceiver, the artist, and the beautification process itself are all aspects of the feminine principle. The creation of concrete forms in which one contemplates the divine is the very reason for the existence of art. The artist as facilitator of manifestation from the invisible into the visible plays two mutually reinforcing roles—as a passive recipient of the idea that is conceived and as an active agent toward that which is to be born. Thus, creativity is the balance between activity and passivity. And as we strive for sustainability, Hafez says, remember that one is in no way superior or inferior to the other.

This view of beauty and manifestation is radically different from the force-based dynamics that characterize much of the industrialized and information stages of human evolution. If Hafez were using modern reference points to put across his teachings, he might use the term "feminine technology" to describe the blend of life-preserving philosophy and appropriate technology that we must construct in the spirit of sustainability.

Such a vital fusion would be an extension of Haféz's philosophy of balance. This equilbrium translates into all forms of wise living on Earth—all practices that temper the speed of technological interconnectedness with deliberate pause for mutual nurturing and that balance the intensely willful competition in the market-place with spiral abandon to spiritual adventure.

When stalemate is achieved and things cannot move, when you go through rapid growth and your outer life moves faster than your inner development, make space, Haféz says. Distance yourself from material achievement in order to gain perspective; do not be afraid that opportunities will slip away or that your competitors will seize what you miss. Instead, reflect on your deeper inner yearnings and unveil your true identity. This way, you repo-sition yourself in the world and thus derive more gratification from your efforts. Remember that if you go up too fast, you also risk coming down just as fast. As with Jamshid, it is not sufficient to simply find the cup; we must also sustain its flow for our own well-being as well as that of all creatures.

Feminine technology requires the courage to enter the dark-ness of the cosmic womb in order to give birth to visionary, sus-tainable, and life-giving ideas and actions. It means stretching our feelings to sense the world in its entirety, to touch the very source of life, to orbit with full focus on the center until we arrive. It exudes unshakable reverence for the sacred, intent for oneness with the wine of generosity and kindness, and authentic joy. Re-member that if we can keep the thread of passion and growth extended through space and time, through thick and thin, the path of evolution will be infinite. Such is the message of the fol-lowing poem.

The Infinite Path

On rendi for years I have walked and still aspire;
greed I imprisoned and obeyed wisdom higher.

The house of Simorgh I did not reach on my own;
I crossed that space with help of Solomon's flier.

Spread shade on my shattered heart, O treasure of love;
I have demolished this house while you I desire.

Repentant, I swore cupbearer's lips not to kiss;
now I bite my own for having listened to liar.

Seek your answers from sources beyond what you're told;
from one stray curl of hair did my wholeness transpire.

Neither you nor I create intoxication;
I did the bidding of great eternity's sire.

That generous sultan promised me paradise
although in the tavern I oft tended the fire.

I thought son Joseph would return when I grew old
to reward my endurance of grief on this pyre.

Early riser and health-seeker such as Haféz
creates his own wealth from the Koran's rich empire.

So if I rise to helm of that tribunal court,
just know that for years I served in that master's hire.

The Wine of Service

At dawn, still half-drunk from the night before,
I drank wine while lute and drum did implore.

I gave mind a final drink for the road
and cast it far from this world's walls and floor.

My wine-selling love glanced seductively,
shielding me from time's misleading uproar.

From curve-browed cupbearer, this warning came:
Condemnation's arrow aims at your door.

Lasso of love will not fit round your waist
if only yourself in loop you adore.

Go spread your net to catch some other bird;
high nest of Simorgh demands that you soar.

Who benefits from goodness of a king
who loves his own face alone evermore?

Steer wine's vessel close so we may pass safe
through stormy sea to invisible shore.

She lives in friend, musician, cupbearer;
tale of water and clay is only lore.

Existence, Haféz, a mystery remains;
probing yields fantasy tales, nothing more.

Service

*T*he purpose of Haféz's poetry is service. The beauty of the
river Roknabad and the garden of Mosalla, the seductive stroll-
ers on the streets of Shiraz, the ruby lips of the beloved, the cup of
wine, and the ecstasy of union are sources of Haféz's inspiration.
His poetry takes the elixir of life from these images and gives
pleasure and guidance to readers and listeners. This natural flow
of give-and-take is the essence of service. Service, Haféz says, is
our link to spirit. It is the act of manifesting in discernible material
forms the abstract qualities of the divine. To the poet, an ultimate
manifestation of the Creator's quality on Earth is the beauty rep-
resented by the feminine. This essence includes the grace of giving
and being egalitarian in one's giving.

The pathway of rendi allows us to build a strong character
through surrender, imagination, competence, courage, and un-
conditional search for truth. These attributes awaken in us the
impulse to project the best of ourselves onto the universe. This
we do without any expectations of particular return and with
complete trust in the process by which our acts of service preserve
the unimaginable continuum of life.

The lineage of Persian mystical poetry began in the ninth century with the master poet Rudaki, who, though blind, was an accomplished harpist. In ancient Middle Eastern myth, a blind harpist opens humanity's auditory sense through an inner vision of metaphysical law. The auditory sense is the direct response to the proportional laws of sound and form, the epistemological basis for science and philosophy. As in other great spiritual cultures of the past, Persian mystics derived their artistic inspiration by participating in the mysterious interaction of the intertwined realities of vibration and form that create life moment after moment.

Haféz, well trained in the art and science of music, was a master at deriving his poetic rhythms from the music of the spheres, the universal harmonies between the primal male and female symbols. In order to perform his act of service—gaining access to and expressing poetry—Haféz blended fully with the archetypes, the world of symbols, the realm of phenomenal worlds, as well as the dark space of shadows. By finding the harmony among cosmic sounds, natural substances, and the creatures of the underworld, the poet was able to create both imaginative language as well as fitting music. As a result, his ghazals have the diverse qualities of nourishing our souls by connecting them to the source of creation, giving us practical perspectives on everyday life by linking us with nature, and making us face our deepest fears and pain.

In order to successfully balance the often contradictory demands of the sacred and profane realms, Haféz says, you must perfect the skill of living and thinking on the razor's edge, without selling yourself to either world:

I speak openly and I happily tell thee:
I am the servant of love—and from both worlds free.

Love is the limitless energy that flows unconditionally between worlds. It is the erotic essence that compels us to fully engage in life and to express our connection and respect for the source of creation through spontaneous acts of service.

Spontaneity—self-aware, instant action—is an essential quality of service. It translates direct perception of spiritual reality into projection of an appropriate material form that mirrors the reality. Service is not something you do sporadically as an obligation or to feel good about yourself or to pay your dues for the privileges and opportunities you have been given. Such convenient service is the way of zahed. The rend, on the other hand, views life itself as service. Every act, thought, and breath resonates with service to the rest of creation. The living process becomes spiritual transformation.

For Haféz, the generosity of the beloved stands as a powerful symbol of service. Every time the world becomes too dark and chaos seduces him to sink into cynicism, the poet recalls the goodness of the beloved. That simple, yet deep flash of memory provides him with inspiration, brings him joy, makes him laugh at the relative smallness of his personal preoccupations, and strengthens his bond with life:

> *Though crop of my life grows from seeds of grief over you,*
> *I swear to dust at your feet my pledge to you endures.*

As Haféz renews his pledge to the beloved, his attachment to the illusion of mastery over nature weakens, and his link to the spirit world is cleansed, preparing him for more liberating service:

> *I swear to friendship: If you take me as servant,*
> *I will rise from mastery of this human stance.*

The word "servant" is not a derogatory term in Haféz's poetry. On the contrary, it connotes the ultimate state of freedom coming from a clear space of surrender and abandon. Echoing the core of Pythagorean theory that frames universal abstractions in measurable terms, Haféz views the level of servitude to life as the most evolved state of the rend. In fact, the very purpose for our being in these finite bodies, Haféz the mystic says, is to discover and manifest supernatural existence within a limited framework. This is our challenge as human beings. Supporting the embodiment of the infinite into the finite is the goal of service.

On the street of rendi they don't buy claim of kinghood;
confess to servitude and give total devotion.

By this definition, service is not a self-righteous act, prone to the danger of heightened arrogance and loss of one's authentic purpose and integrity of intention:

I want not the stone of Solomon's ring, even for free,
for at times Ahriman's hands have touched its precious magic.

In Hafez's poetry, we are offered the wisdom of realizing that there is always someone else and something else in a more challenging situation than we are. This means that everyone, no matter in what condition, can be of service to others and to society:

Although I am dusty, my effort shames my poverty;
my work must propel more fuel to the light before I'm done.

Though in poverty, I hold a kingly treasure in hand;
why covet the petty fortune that by the fates is won?

Despite my poverty, may I become dark-faced like Moon
when I gaze at luminosity of fortunate Sun.

In this view, the strict hierarchy of those who have and those who have not dissolves. Instead, it gives way to a new global community of guests, challenged to be joyful, skillful, celebrative, passionate, bridge-building, and laughing children of creation. In this vision, we know that we have always been servants of life and will always be so, no matter how many times we pass through this earthly realm:

I am a servant and poor, but I would not exchange
my woolen hat for the offer of a hundred crowns.

Service is the primordial intent of the rend, the warrior of life. It is the flow of doing what you can, to the best of your ability, in order to bring forth the potentiality in abstract forms that desire to become and manifest in concrete reality. As such, service encompasses the process of creation. In poetic terms, it requires three important tools: clear listening (to the universe's repertoire of symphonies in order to detect which pieces wish to be heard and when), stretching of the intellect (done with both rigor and vigor in order to expand imagination for creative visioning and expression), and particular skills (in imagery and writing used diligently to bring forth that music). These same tools also apply to art, science, education, and business.

Service is the intent and perseverance with which we perfect and apply these tools. Service, the pure water running freely through the ocean of generosity, is blind to appearances of profit and loss. We give because giving is how life begins:

My monastery in tavern corner lies;
my mantra is prayer to Elder of skies.

If morning breeze and lyre make no sound, don't fear;
my song at dawn is a repentance of sighs.

I am free of both pauper and king, thank God,
for begging at beloved's door is my prize.

Serving, to me, is greater than sultancy;
passion and longing is the path I advise.

From the time I first opened this tavern door,
my leaning place warmed at the height of Sun's rise.

In Middle Eastern spirituality, the beginning of life revealed two tendencies as the source of creative tension. On the one hand, the cosmos moved in the direction of the infinite—the ocean of sound and light and vibration. On the other hand, it gravitated toward the finite—the world of concrete solutions and objectives, as in water, earth, fire, and air.

Embodying in a balanced way this combination of abstract forms and specific elements is the basis of selfless and relevant service. It is relevant because it embraces the entirety of the universe within which all creatures live. It is selfless because it must remove ego—the barrier of the mind—from the flow between the servant and that which is the source of service. As Haféz asks us to ponder in the poem "The Wine of Service," at the beginning of this chapter:

Who benefits from goodness of a king
who loves his own face alone evermore?

Service is not the one-sided movement of one part giving and another part receiving but rather a process of mutual give-and-take. Therefore, Haféz says:

Steer wine's vessel close so we may pass safe
through stormy sea to invisible shore.

Blending the worlds of the limitless and the limited into a life-nurturing and sustaining balance is the transformative quality of service. Transformation is the process by which an object changes form—it moves from one essence into something else.

Middle Eastern teachings share the world's ancient vision of a vibratory process of physical creation. As in the Sanskrit seed sound *om,* which is said to create rippling vibrations through the universe, the divine word *rahim* (compassionate) is similarly intended as a call for creation in Sufi mysticism. In this context, the purpose of compassion is to give an archetypal form the possibility of receiving sensate existence, thus transforming it from an abstract entity into concrete existence.

The subtle act of facilitating such transformation is at the core of service. In service, we become an agent of change, an instrument by which the divine can have a vision of self in another form. Two tensions allow the process of service and transformation to take place: the desire of the invisible form to be known and the preparedness of the visible to embody the invisible. In Persian imagery, this phenomenon is often represented by the imagery of a potter's vision and the clay used in the artistic process. The artisan both perceives a particular archetype ready to be actualized in the sentient world and also gauges the readiness of the clay to take that form.

To be successful, this highly delicate process requires two complementary levels of awareness. On the one hand, it demands an impeccable sense of timing on the part of the artist. Making the pottery before the clay is ready to absorb the intent of the archetype would result in a less than excellent piece of work. Making it too late would fail to capture the potency of the synchronous fusion between the will of the invisible and the preparedness of the clay. This subtle sense of timing is tied to the second level of awareness required in the creative service process: self-knowledge on the part of the artisan, the agent of change. Without self-knowledge, the artist misses the signals of potentiality and the precise openings for action.

The intuitive connection with one's authentic self results from the gathering of one's spiritual faculties, often symbolized by birds in the Sufi tradition. This gathering, a metaphor for khater-e majmou, is well illustrated in the Persian poet Attar's "Conference of the Birds," a mystical work much admired by Haféz.

This beautiful story told through rhythmic poems builds on a Koranic verse in which Solomon announces that "we have been taught the language of the birds, and all favors have been showered upon us." The hoopoe, Solomon's flier and the symbol of divine inspiration, assembles a flock of diverse birds in order to search for Simorgh, the most evolved of all birds. As Haféz explains:

> *The house of Simorgh I did not reach on my own;*
> *I crossed that space with help of Solomon's flier.*

The flock embarks on a journey during which each bird sings a different tune, many trying to delay the quest by bringing up the pain of separating from their worldly attachments. Only those birds that can see beyond the material realm and awaken to their inner dimensions succeed in reaching the goal of completion. At the end of the journey, all the birds discover that the truth of Simorgh was within themselves all along.

One reason for the depth of self-knowing required of the

agent of service is the need to build the single most important tool necessary in the creative process—the capacity for deep listening. Without this auditory ability to perceive clearly, to distinguish false voices from the authentic voice representing both the self and the archetype that intends to become known, the catalyst of transformation may engage in utterly futile and potentially damaging acts. Service, by definition, is constructive. It is a movement of complete clarity, spontaneity, competence, and awareness of all dimensions of existence.

To be an effective catalyst in the creation of freedom for others, we first free ourselves from the pull of the ego. Transcending our limiting minds, breaking the walls of separation, and melting with complete abandon into the rest of creation are the required actions for engaging in service:

> In rends' neighborhood they buy only broken hearts;
> market of ego-selling is the other way.

The spiritual cleansing process, also termed "polishing the mirror" in Persian mysticism, allows us to hear distinctly the will of the invisible force that intends to be born. By fully blending and becoming one with that force, we allow its will to link with our own, thus generating a powerful fire of inspiration and passion that brings forth the invisible into manifestation. This unity of intent, the synchronicity between the servant and the source of service, leads to the blissful fluidity of joy as a by-product of synchronous service.

This fluidity also requires that communion with the spirit world take place in a way that supports the individuation process. Otherwise, you run the danger of losing your true self to the dizzying diversity of the archetypal world. Such loss of individual integrity, Haféz warns, can easily convert the ecstatically grounded rend into a disoriented debauchee incapable of manifestation and frustrated by repressed creativity. The need for full individuation in the midst of fusion with others is at the heart of humanity's challenge as the global community becomes more intricately linked through trade, travel, and information exchange. But our ability to perform sustainable acts of service on the evolutionary path resides in our effectiveness in balancing the process of strengthening the integrity of individual entities with our efforts at community building.

As the people of the new millennium transform their personal, family, and organizational lives within the interconnected web of the global society, Haféz urges us to transcend the most debilitating barrier that prevents us from engaging in and deriving pleasure from the spirit of service: self-centered complaint:

> *I am not one ever to groan from disunity;*
> *I am devotee and servant seeking completion.*

In our lives, whether at home or in organizations, Haféz would advise us to become one with the purpose of the whole environment. Love what you do, no matter what it is, and know that every task is an opportunity for transcendence, a fulfilling flow of give-and-take. Even if you work with people whose values do not match yours, remember that you can have complete affinity with the work that you do. Your pact is with the spirit, not with those who hire you:

> *Loyalty to self is excellent, you will learn;*
> *otherwise, you will be swayed by others' needing.*

> *Don't be a slave to earnings as mendicants are;*
> *Haféz himself knows well the way of slave-breeding.*

Service is an oath with the Creator, a voluntary agreement to sustain the evolution of humanity and all other species:

> *The purpose of mosque and tavern is union with you;*
> *I have no other thing in mind, God is my witness.*

When the larger environment within which we live and work appears alienating, when banality becomes oppressive, we can connect our breath with the infinite flow of life and take responsibility for touching the inspirational presence of abundance that is always within reach. The mind that fears annihilation by scarcity will vanish. It will metamorphose into a drive for risk-taking and a vision of plenitude that will further fuel our will for unconditional service:

> *If we are unable to reach and touch your long hair,*
> *it is the failure of our confusion and short hand.*

Faced with the adversity of condemnation and cynicism threatening to weaken our will, we listen to these sobering words:

> *Beyond sarcasm, even if enemy pokes me with blade,*
> *I will hold beloved close; whatever happens, happens.*

Our ability to surmount the seductively repressive tendencies of the world will, in turn, strengthen our self-confidence and determination to stay with an intended purpose:

> *I swear, if the whole world appears in my mind,*
> *my desire for your goodness will not lessen.*

With joy, self-determination, focus, and perseverance, the wine of service flows, and the mystery takes care of you, the servant:

> *Those who choose to side with God's creatures—*
> *the Creator will protect them from harm.*

Haféz warns, however, that while breathing comfort into our souls, service is not an offering in return for or in expectation of self-centered power. We serve justice, peace, and the web of creation, regardless of whether the wheel of life turns our way at any given time:

> *Don't think that from the dust of your doorway I will*
> *oppose fate of heavens and tyranny of time.*

Here, refusing to oppose the "tyranny of time" is not a withdrawal or an apolitical position of apathy. Haféz, with his masterly diplomacy and political acumen, would not recommend withdrawal from the world or indifference to oppressive forces. What he mirrors in this significant couplet is the inner nobility of surrender coupled with efficient singularity of vision as called for by circumstances. In today's terminology, we refer to this dual art as "strategic posturing with integrity."

The poet's keen eye for the critical role of purposeful resignation —a sophisticated form of risk-taking—in effecting long-term objectives is illustrated by his handling of one particular political situation in the province of Fars. A few years before Haféz's death, Shiraz was invaded by Timur (also known as Tamerlane), the fierce Central Asian conqueror so notorious for violence that he is remembered as the "Scourge of God." Haféz wrote a famous ghazal that is still recited today by Iranians as an example of the poet's political farsightedness. The phrase "Shirazi Turk" is offered as a double compliment of beauty and friendship to the invading Timur:

> *If that Shirazi Turk can capture my heart and my soul,*
> *I'd give Samarghand and Bokhara for his black slave's mole.*

Samarghand and Bokhara are two major cities in today's Russian province of Tajikistan, once part of ancient Iran. With the allegory of exchanging two key territories for a slave's mole, Haféz both announces his desire to see a peaceful Timur capable of capturing the poet's heart and acknowledges its lack of probability— two cities for one mole is a highly unlikely exchange.

At this same time, bitter and violent internal struggles within the ruling Al-e-Mozaffar dynasty of Fars reached new heights. But Mansur Shah, the last king of the dynasty, resisted Timur's military advances and also increased political freedom and raised economic prosperity. As a gesture of goodwill toward the powerful shah from his nation's best-known poet, Haféz wrote a twenty-five-verse poem to Mansur in brilliant, biluminous phrasing that leaves the reader uncertain as to whether the poet is addressing God or the king. In his detached rendi way, he ends the poem with this famous couplet:

> *The purpose of this poetic exchange is to humor you;*
> *my inspiration is not for sale, and I don't buy coyness.*

As Haféz continued to watch the political situation, he

observed that despite Mansur Shah's willful resistance, there was no critical mass capable of withstanding a major intervention by Timur. The shah stood as a singularly strong tree in the path of a potentially devastating torrent of invading forces. Haféz understood the futility of untimely and uncoordinated war and the importance of an expanded mind capable of seeing the bigger picture. About three years before his own death, he wrote a long poem that is now called "Saghinameh" (Epic of the Cupbearer), considered one of his finest works. With the lucid warning that "destiny is planning to create a calamity," Haféz began a chain of invocations concerning the potential downfall of the ruling dynasty. Future events in Persian history proved so many of his commentaries correct that scholars now cite the epic as a demonstration of the poet's political genius.

A few years after Haféz's death, Timur took over Shiraz, killed Mansur Shah, mass-murdered other members of the ruling family, and set off a bloody chain of terror. Over time, it took the clever and nonviolent tactics of those whom Haféz would call rends to weaken the tides of oppression in Persia and pave the way for freer times to return. The story of these rends and their visionary posture illustrates clearly Haféz's notion of strategic timing and tactics.

One of these rends was the Sufi mystic Ali Ardebili, whose story has been called "The Sanctuary with Two Doors." Ali managed a monastery for the poor that his grandfather, the noted Sufi master Sheikh Safi-ud-Din Ardebili, had founded in the city of Ardebil in northwestern Iran in the early fourteenth century. A few years after Haféz's death, Timur captured and transported thirty thousand Persian prisoners of war to Ardebil. There, Ali met with Timur and asked for the release of as many prisoners as could enter his small monastery. Swayed by Ardebili's negotiation skills, Timur agreed.

According to the story, as quickly as the prisoners entered the sanctuary, Ardebili guided them out through the back door. As a result, all thirty thousand passed into the monastery and onward to freedom. Subsequently, many prisoners regained their prosperity and leadership positions and became loyal supporters of Ardebili's mystic way. A century after Timur's death, the descendants of the freed prisoners helped the seventh-generation grandson of Safi-ud-Din Ardebili found the Safavid dynasty. Following the mystical path of their ancestry, the Safavids created one of the world's great legacies in art, education, and architecture.

When it comes to strategic posturing in service, Haféz's message is clear: Adopt the clever way of the farsighted deer rather than the aggressive force of the roaring lion. Don't groan and show off your might for short-term gains. Instead, be smart and vigilant, listen clearly to every sound around you, charm with your grace, know how to run fast and silently, and be ready to hide when necessary in order to get a better view of the landscape and plan your next move. Sometimes, being a quiet strategist behind the scenes is more effective than parading loudly on the front line:

> *Don't set foot on love's street without clear motivation;*
> *whoever doesn't learn fully on this path will fail.*

> *The wonders of walking rendi, O friend, are many;*
> *facing deer of this desert, the roaring lion turned tail.*

In these couplets, the poet imparts the valuable counsel that focused gentleness is power. This is Haféz's own gateway to spiritual growth and worldly fulfillment, and it is his message to us, the humanity of the Information Age, as we search for peace and impactful service. This wisdom also paves the way for part 4 of this book, a quest for vision and meaning in the poem "The Wild Deer," Haféz's intimate masterpiece of his final years.

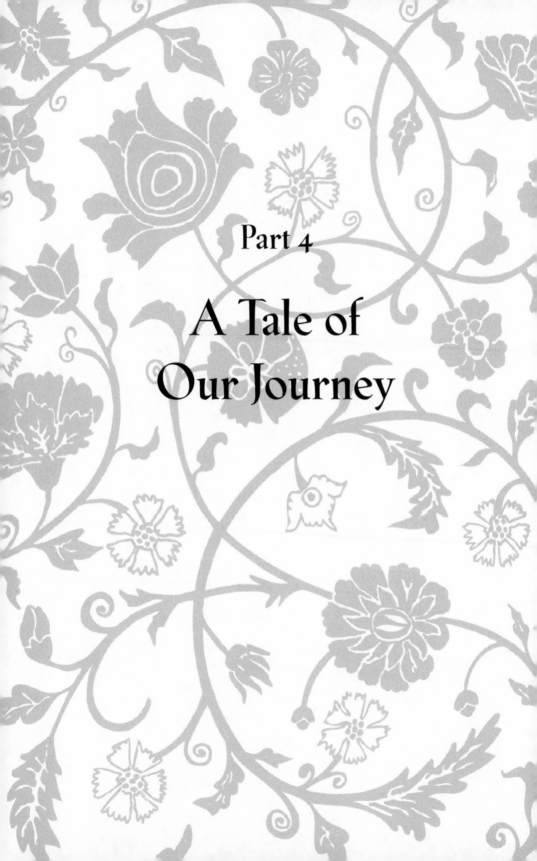

Part 4

A Tale of
Our Journey

The Elder Takes His Leave

*L*ate in life, Haféz composed "The Wild Deer," a marvelous poem of passage often honored as his masterpiece. In this poem, Haféz invites us to join him during his last years, to listen to him as a fulfilled human being on the verge of the silent depths of death, and to participate in his joy and eternal longing as he ponders his magnificent harvest of life.

Iranian scholar Dr. Mohammad Ali Islami Nadoushan calls Haféz "the master of transforming specifics to whole and whole to specifics." He writes: "If we were to put our finger on one work that more than any other synthesizes the essence of Haféz's mood and that serves as an autobiography, we would be talking about 'The Wild Deer.' We see this *masnavi* linked to Haféz's old age and perhaps the very end of his life."[17] The masnavi is a poetic story form longer than the ghazal and distinguished by the rhyming of both lines of each couplet. The mastery of the poet emerges in the alignment, attunement, and harmony of all elements of the composition. Through the finely grained picture of the wild deer, the poet reveals his vision of the transitory nature of life.

To Haféz, the two worlds of existence were perceived through humanity's six senses, the sixth organ of sensory perception being the soul itself, with poetry as the stimulus of the soul. This corresponds to the eye beholding the beauty of the beloved, the ear hearing the music of the spheres, the tongue tasting the sweetness of wine, the skin shivering from sensual touch, and the nose embracing intoxication from the scent of musk. In poetry, the West Wind of Persian history sometimes carries this fragrance of musk, the enticing perfume extracted from an organ in the belly of the deer. The best musk of the time was imported from China, and Persians often wore musk in their collars or in a small container hanging from a cord around the neck. Throughout the *Divan,* poignant couplets focus on both the deer and this deep internal fragrance. For instance:

> *O hunter, don't kill that musk-bearing deer of mine;*
> *be moved by that dark eye and don't take him in prey.*

The wild deer is Haféz's twin companion—or double—in thought, spirit, and action. No other animal or companion would have satisfied the landscape of qualities esteemed by Haféz as the wild deer does. The poet speaks with the wild deer within a space of infinite delicacy of thought and feeling because he has found his double. The Farsi phrase is *ham nafas*—someone with whom you are so closely bound that you seem to breathe the same spiritual air. The two beings perceive, think, and feel in astonishingly similar ways. Haféz develops this allegory by aligning imagery and words with the depth of mysticism, painting an imaginative portrait of his own feelings and visions through the wild deer.

In the following couplet taken from another ghazal, the poet expresses the intricate connection between humans and animals through the unity of compassion. The essence expressed is that which he sought all his life and experienced in complete fulfillment during his last years:

> *If the fragrance of joy flows from the blood of my heart,*
> *don't be surprised; I also feel pain from deer's musk bag.*

This verse describes Haféz's sustained thread of relationship with the wild deer. His direct expression of deep affinity is mirrored by the deer's own presence throughout the mythology of Persia and virtually all other ancient cultures. In India, for instance, legend tells that the first sermon preached by the Buddha was in the Deer Park at Benares, where in a previous existence he had incarnated as a golden deer in order to protect his herd from the hunters of the king and bring freedom for all sentient beings.

In Iran today, the very first poem known to be written in the Farsi language was about the wild deer. This verse, which goes back more than one thousand one hundred years, was composed by Abu Hafs Soghdi. He wrote of the wild deer and its universal image of solitary existence in the wide world:

See how the wild deer runs in the desert free;
he runs alone and friendless—how can this be?

In Islamic tradition, one of the most honored religious leaders is Imam Reza, commonly known as the Eighth Imam. Each year, more than eleven million Shiite pilgrims visit his shrine in Mashad in Eastern Iran and address this eighth-century holy man as the "guardian of the deer." Like Haféz, the Eighth Imam was a highly learned and clairvoyant man who spent the last years of his life under jealous attack by politicians and religious nemeses. He died in a foreign land from poisonous grapes given to him by a jealous prince. Researchers attribute the connection between the imam and the deer to the synthesized imagery of a very smart being who is isolated and targeted by deadly blows. The pilgrims' cry to the "guardian of the deer" is a call for guidance to those who are lonely, live as refugees, and are caught in the net of fear and anxiety.

In order to present Haféz's "The Wild Deer" in its most accessible form to modern readers, we have divided the poem into four distinct "acts": The Quest, Seeds, Life and Death, and The Legacy. We also are offering two versions of each act, one following the other. The first version is a poetry translation in the style of the ghazals. The second is a prose interpretation delivered in language such as the poet might use were he to improvise a monologue in contemporary English.

In Act One: The Quest, Haféz introduces Wild Deer as his ham nafas, the ultimate of intimacy. He begins a contemplative dialogue with himself, then brings the reader into his fold, inviting us to listen to his innermost thoughts, to take a panoramic view of his quest, and to share with him the joy of harvesting the mature fruits of his life.

As Haféz's memory flashes back, an enthusiastic but inexperienced youth confronts the lessons of life in Act Two: Seeds. You must sow in order to harvest, an experienced farmer tells the youth. One must start with the desire to plant the seed meticulously, care for it, become one with it, then reap the yield. But the youth replies: I want to soar and find the great teacher Simorgh and embody the light, heat, and generosity of the Sun's infinite energy. This is how my soul must evolve. This is my way.

In Act Three: Life and Death, Haféz depicts the passing caravan of life. Perhaps he is remembering a dear one who has passed—a son, wife, or friend—or perhaps he is speaking of his wild deer guide and double. Or it may be simply life in general—his life on this Earth. The caravan conveys the imagery of a long trip, bringing separation that creates sadness. Now Haféz becomes so intimate that he allows you to see his tears. As the river of life increases in speed and movement, he says that you, too, must increase the flowing water of your eye proportionately. This is the tear of pain from separation that we all share. It is a cleansing element that can facilitate entrance into a cathartic state of surrender and spiritual ablution. This cleansing, Haféz explains with the hard-earned wisdom of an elder who embodies balance of thought and spirit, will allow you to stretch body and mind and to dance with the ever-challenging wheel of life. This, the poet promises us, is our only healing medication against the tyranny of time. This section is a call for reflection through a dramatic language designed to jolt us and bring our attention to the importance of life and death. He pleads with the masses—who, as Moslems, are sincere truth-seekers—to echo the name of God and evoke its true essence.

Act Four: The Legacy is about reaping the yield from planted seeds. In the last years of his life, in particular, Haféz was bothered by Shiraz's charlatans, who insisted on soiling his name or even passing off their own poems as his. He opens this final act by advising that we must distinguish between the true and the false voices of life. He declares that his authentic poetry will stand the test of time and that it elicits the same divine call for perseverance as *noon-ol-ghalam,* the message God sent to Mohammad advising the Prophet not to worry about people's fears that his inspired oratory was madness. Haféz explains that the fusion of mind and spirit has been his goal, and the elixir of this fusion is the yield of kindness, friendship, and justice to be harvested at the end of his life.

The final couplet serves as Haféz's will to humanity and society. It is composed of simple, delicately expressed imagery of life and death. As the poet sees death approaching, he bequeaths a message: Beware, this temporary existence on Earth is only a step away from death. All is fragile and all is precious. Live in the present and appreciate it to the fullest.

On the following pages are the four acts of "The Wild Deer," with the prose interpretations of each act on the page facing the translated poem.

The Wild Deer

Act One

O Wild Deer, my old friend, where are you today?
So much like each other, we've come all this way.

Lonely and wandering, we two cannot last;
we are both prey stalked by our future and past.

So let us into one another inquire
and discover therein our deepest desire.

Why cannot these depths of our wild desert land
offer safety and joy sometimes in its sand?

Who to our rescue? O lovers, time to speak,
you companions of sorrow and strangers weak.

We need a great miracle—Khezr must arrive;
perhaps our journey's end his grace will contrive.

The time has come for the faithful to appear;
so stay, friend, hear a tale of our journey here.

The Quest

My autumn arrives. Time travels through me and change
encroaches on this season of my soul. I am the poet of two
worlds, it is said, but I am a man of one body. What now that I
must release this human form? O Wild Deer—my spirit self—
how do we two travel on? What will become of me? Of you?

Our freedom measured by memory and destiny, we seek
answer in each other's mirrored self. But grief, not joy, thrives
in these shadowed mirrors of passage. We seek comfort from
companions—but none answers. Our only hope is a miracle
from Khezr, the life-giver—a miracle to light the separate
pathways to our journey's end.

But, my dear friend and reader, this is not where this story
begins. So come and listen. Let me tell you of a poet's quest for
wholeness, a tale of this journey of life.

Act Two

This story began far away and long ago
when master asked youth what soul seeks to know:

Young quester, what's in that bag on your shoulder?
If wisdom seed, plant; reap as you grow older.

Youth replied: Yes, such a seed do I carry
but only Simorgh can answer my query.

Elder then warned: That goal is a great test;
there is no worldly place Simorgh builds its nest.

I know, said the youth, to fail may be my fate,
but life with no hope is a far greater weight.

I desire a note not in tune with your key;
light and fire from the Sun must harmonize me.

So long as I breathe, this way will I think;
so long as cup's offered, that long will I drink.

Seeds

In youth, I sought to know myself. The learned elder advised:
Listen, little one, go slow, and all will be well. Plant your seeds
deep, cultivate patience, reap the yield as the wisdom of years.
This way, in time, you will understand all.

But my wild desire replied: Well and good for you, but an
ancient pulse drives my heart, and a luminous flame sears my
mind. My soul is Simorgh, and it must soar to the heavens of
our beginning and end. I shall risk all. I shall surrender to
that ancient ebb and flow of fiery rays, for the dark eye of
creation is my heartbeat, and the throbbing of cosmic will
gives me hope. Only the Sun's vibrant glow can slake my
thirst for essence.

And in this way I split myself into two: I as the laboring man
of words, my spirit as the unbridled deer of vision. Together,
we became the poet, breathing the life of inspiration,
sharing the wine of intoxication.

Act Three

Thus begun, caravan claims cypress and all;
whatever eye sees must return journey's call.

Hold firm the wine cup and also the flower,
but see as well wheel of life's final power.

Beside our source, you sit next to a river;
a single tear falls, you feel the soul shiver.

Remembering friends passed and those still alive,
we ascend to spring clouds and there we all thrive.

But river runs fast, then more rapidly still;
the grasp of our vision must catch today's thrill.

My old companion another road has trod;
O Moslems, Moslems, call the true name of God.

Death's sad blade that separates all who do live
leaves us strangers as though no love did we give.

Companion goes from me and my heart does grieve;
brother to brother only sorrow does leave.

Now only a miracle of Khezr can mend
and unite lonely me and my lonely friend.

Life and Death

We all journey on this passing caravan in accord with the
wheel of life's eternal turning. While treasuring beauty and
wisdom, we understand the mortality of even the cypress. To
sit still and feel life's flow within the soul is to unleash tears of
this sadness, and in reverie we ache for friends already flown
to the clouds. In our dream, life and death seem as one.

But time's river rushes on and I must face its flow anew. My
heart's companion—that one who is me and yet also is not—
departs. We turn from brothers to strangers. Burning with
grief, I cry out: O my people, all my dear ones, let us embrace
the true reality of the Creator. Our final union exists only in
return to the source where we—even my deer and I—can be
brought together again.

This is the miracle, Khezr, for which I pray.

Act Four

Perceive the jewel and pass by the glass bead;
let go the pathway that does not to light lead.

My pen goes to writing as Jonah to whale,
as noon-ol-ghalam inspired words beyond veil.

I've mixed spirit and mind and seeded my field;
that my vision's seen is the fruit of my yield.

Pure rapture arises when fusion is goal
of beauty of poem and essence of soul.

From the fragrance of all this sweet-scented rhyme,
let perfume wash over your soul throughout time.

Such musk comes from necks of angels of Cathay,
not from the Wild Deer who from me fades away.

Friends, value each other, we can't know what's next;
don't try to memorize, don't read from the text.

This counselor's wisdom now has been told;
comes the stone-thrower of death as I grow old.

The Legacy

That is my story, and now I've grown old. I speak as elder—
but be aware; you must awaken fully to appreciate the value of
this jewel. Through my pen—inspired like the Prophet's
oration—flows the wisdom of both spirit and body, both Wild
Deer and me. My earthly seeds yield vision through union of
soul and message, and from this elixir exudes an intoxicating
musk for the ages. True, spirit touches us from the sacred
realm, but it's the sweet verse of humanity that blesses this
world. Here, then, I say:

Dear friend and reader, treasure each breath of this life.
Embrace and love, for there are no other constants. You need
search no further. You need not memorize holy words as I did.
You need not recite sacred writings. I have lived at the source,
this simplicity is my counsel, it is offered freely, and I've no
more to say. Now my human death—that old stone-thrower—
is creeping closer. But I walk on. I do not despair,
for reunion awaits—and therein as well,
Wild Deer, my old friend.

I saw new moon's sickle rise in the green field of sky,
remembered time to harvest my own seed draws nigh.

I scolded fate: You went to sleep and missed the sunrise.
Fate replied: Don't fret, Sun will rise again by and by.

Notes

Introduction

1. Boylan, *Hafez: Dance of Life,* 3.
2. Boylan, *Hafez: Dance of Life,* translation of quote by Michael C. Hillman, 95. Original source: Javdaneh Forugh Farrokhzad (Immortal Forugh Farrokhzad), published in Iran.
3. Goethe, *West-Östlicher Divan: West-Eastern Divan,* 31.
4. Emerson, "Journals of 1847," *The Complete Works of Ralph Waldo Emerson,* 1903, Vol. 8, 31.
5. Bell, *The Teachings of Hafiz,* 88.
6. Khan, *The Hand of Poetry,* 136.
7. Ibid., 144.
8. Smith, *Hafiz: Tongue of the Hidden,* 14.

Part 1

Jamshid's Biluminous Cup

9. Nietzsche, *Der Wille Zùr Macht* (The Will To Power), translated by Ali-Gholi Mahmoudi Bakhtiari in *Rahi be Maktab-e Haféz* (A Path to the School of Haféz), 30.

10. *Sumer: Cities of Eden,* 1993, 148.
11. Mehr, *The Zoroastrian Tradition,* 38.

Part 2

A Choice of Mythology

12. Shaw, *Man and Superman,* 32.

Part 3

The Big Picture

13. Resolution by United Nations Educational, Scientific and Cultural Organization (UNESCO), November, 1987, commemorating the 600th anniversary of the death of the Iranian poet Haféz.
14. Hillmann (Boylan, *Hafez: Dance of Life,* 95) writes: "In this view, she [Forugh Farrokhzad] echoes the words of Nima Yushij (1895–1960), the 'father' of modern Persian poetry, who acknowledges Hafez's deserved preeminence and laments the fact that Iran has always had so few *sha'ers* (true poets) and so many *nazems* (versifiers)."
15. Payne, *The Poems of Shemseddin Mohammad Hafiz of Shiraz,* vol. 1.

Sustainability

16. Whitemore, *The Best of Friends,* 60.

Part 4

The Elder Takes His Leave

17. Islami Nadoushan, *Majaraye Pyar Napazire Haféz (The Endless Adventure of Haféz),* 304–305.

Farsi (Persian) Glossary

Attar   Twelfth- and thirteenth-century Persian poet. Composer of the "Conference of the Birds."

Avesta   "The Hymns of Zarathustra." A book of verses composed by the founder of Zoroastrianism.

Avicenna   Eleventh-century philosopher who lived in Tehran.

divan (Divan)   Literally, a collection. Used uppercase in this book, it refers to the collection of Haféz's poetry that is now the Middle East's best-known divination tool. There are many different editions.

Estakhr   City where Alexander the Great destroyed the original Avesta.

Ghaem Magham Farahani   Creator of the contemporary Farsi prose form—an evolutionary, efficient, rhythmic prose that became a writing model for many prominent Iranian novelists in the twentieth century. Ghaem Magham was an influential statesman during the reign of three kings in the Ghajar dynasty. He was murdered by political enemies while serving as Iran's chancellor in 1835.

Forugh Farrokhzad   Contemporary (1935–67) poet and one of Iran's best-known female literary figures.

Fars   An Iranian province. Shiraz is the capital.

filsouf   Philosopher.

ghazal   Lyric poetry form with stylized rhythmic and rhyming schemes. Raised to its highest level by Saadi and Haféz in Shiraz.

Hafézieh   The mausoleum of Haféz at Mosalla garden, Shiraz.

ham nafas   One's spiritual double, someone so close that both beings seem to breathe the same spiritual air.

houri   A nymph of Paradise.

iham   A Persian literary technique of comparison involving wordplay, sound association, and double meanings.

imam   Shiite Moslem religious leader.

Imam Reza   Eighth-century religious leader known as the Eighth Imam. Known to Shiite Moslems as the "guardian of the deer."

Jamshid's Cup   The chalice of life's secrets; in Persian poetry, the same as the Holy Grail. Jamshid (Jam) was a mythical king of ancient Persia.

Kay Khosrow   An ancient Persian king descended from Jamshid.

Khaneghah   A Sufi monastery in Persia.

khater-e majmou   The gathered memory. A clearly focused awareness of one's thoughts, emotions, and personality traits, resulting in a condition of inner peace.

Khayyam, Omar   Eleventh-century mathematician and poet, made famous by Edward Fitzgerald's nineteenth-century translation of his rubaiyat.

Khezr   One of the most honored figures in Middle Eastern mythology. A worker of miracles, identified with the sea and with the greenery of nature. Corresponds to the Biblical prophet Elijah.

Lessan-ul-Gheib   Arabic name for Haféz—"Tongue of the Unseen."

Mansur, Shah   Shiraz ruler who played a major role in some of Haféz's later poems.

Mashad   City in eastern Iran. Site of the religious shrine of Imam Reza.

masnavi   A lyric poem, longer than the ghazal. The lines of each couplet rhyme.

Mazdaism   The religion preceding Zoroastrianism in ancient Persia.

mehr   The Sun.

mehrab   The domed hut of the ancient mystery schools of Iran. Its ceiling was painted with the Moon and stars to simulate the universe, and the doorway faced east. In current usage, an altar, prayer house, or place of worship.

Mithra   In ancient Persian mythology, the celestial emissary who served as the Lord of Justice.

mogh   A seeker in the ancient Persian religious tradition. The plural is *moghan*.

Mohammad Attar   According to legend, Haféz's spiritual teacher in Shiraz. He was said to be a merchant.

mohtasseb   A sheriff. In Haféz's poetry, he is the enforcer of the puritanical laws imposed by the social establishment.

Mosalla   A garden on the periphery of Shiraz, site of Hafézieh.

nazem   A versifier: one who writes verse that basically reflects traditional form and content.

noon-ol-ghalam   In the Koran, God's message that inspired Mohammad to go on with his work. The message told the Prophet not to be distracted when people feared him because of his inspired and unmatched oratory.

Norouz   The Iranian New Year, which begins on the first day of spring.

Persepolis   Capital of the ancient Persian Empire.

Pir-e-Moghan   The evolved, timeless being known as the Elder.

Pir-e-Sabz   The Green Man, another form of Khezr.

rahim   Compassionate.

Ramadan   The Islamic month of fasting.

rebec   A stringed musical instrument in the violin family.

rend   In usual usage, a debauchee. In Haféz's terminology, a spiritual warrior, someone who takes a nonordinary path to enlightenment.

rendi   The spiritual pathway of the rend, the spiritual warrior.

Roknabad   The beautiful river of Shiraz.

rubaiyat   The four-line poetry form made famous by Edward Fitzgerald's translation of the works of Omar Khayyam.

Rudaki   The blind, harp-playing, ninth-century poet who began the literary lineage that peaked with Haféz.

Rumi, Jalal-ud-Din   Thirteenth-century Sufi mystic and poet who founded the Molavi order of dervishes.

Saadi   Thirteenth-century poet of Shiraz who was a master of the ghazal and an inspiration for Haféz.

Safavid   Ruling dynasty of the fifteenth to eighteenth century, during which Persian culture flourished.

Saghinameh   "Epic of the Cup Bearer." A title given to one of Haféz's later poems.

seé sadr   Arabic word connoting an expansion of one's perspective and being. Literally, "expanded chest."

Shaaban   The month preceding Ramadan.

sha'er   A true poet: a creative artist whose form and content unify to project a unique vision.

shahed   The witness. When seeking a divinatory message from the *Divan,* a second poem (immediately following the first) is read to expand the meaning of the first. This second poem is said to be the witness, corroborating the guidance.

Shakh-e-Nabat   "Branch of Sugarcane." In legend, the woman whose image inspired Haféz on a forty-night vision quest.

shayyadan   The Shiraz neighborhood where Haféz is said to have been born. Literally, charlatans, imposters.

Sheherazad   Arabic name of the heroine of the story "One Thousand and One Nights" in the classic *Tales of the Arabian Nights.*

sheikh   Arabic for spiritual master.

Shiraz   The home city of Haféz, located now in southern Iran.

Simorgh   The mystical bird that possesses the highest spiritual wisdom in Attar's "Conference of the Birds" and other Persian literature.

tabalvor-e mozaaf Biluminosity. A term describing Haféz's unique and ingenious technique of embodying simultaneous enlightenment from both divine and worldly sources in his poetry.

Tehran Capital city of Iran.

vahdat Unity.

yeganeh Unity, wholeness.

zahed In usual usage, a devout person. In the terminology of Haféz, a pious, zealous, self-righteous, self-serving fundamentalist—the opposite of rend.

Zarathustra Founder of the ancient religion now known by the Greek term Zoroastrianism.

Selected English Bibliography

Arberry, A. J. *Classical Persian Literature.* London: Ruskin House, 1938.
———. *Fifty Poems of Hafiz.* London: Curzon Press, 1947.
Aryanpur Kashani, Abbas. *Odes of Hafiz: Poetical Horoscope.* Lexington, Ky.: Mazda, 1984.
Attar, Farid ud-Din. *The Conference of the Birds: A Sufi Fable.* Translation by C. S. Nott. Boston: Shambhala, 1993.
Bakhtiar, Laleh. *Sufi: Expressions of the Mystic Quest.* New York: Avon, 1976.
Bell, Gertrude. *Teachings of Hafiz.* London: Octagon Press, 1979; original publication, 1897.
Bayat, Mojdeh, and Jamnia, Mohammad Ali. *Tales from the Land of the Sufis.* Boston: Shambhala, 1994.
Boylan, Michael (poetry translator). *Hafez: Dance of Life.* Washington D.C.: Mage, 1988.
Brown, E. G. *A Literary History of Persia.* 4 vols. Cambridge: Cambridge University Press, 1964.
Campbell, Joseph. *The Masks of God.* Hammondsworth, UK: Penguin, 1982.
———. *The Inner Reaches of Outer Space.* New York: Harper and Row, 1988.

Curtis, Vesta Sarkhosh. *Persian Myths: The Legendary Past.* Austin: University of Texas, 1993.

Duchesne-Guillemin, Jacques. *The Hymns of Zarathustra.* Boston: Beacon Press, 1963.

Emerson, Ralph Waldo. *The Complete Works of Ralph Waldo Emerson.* Vol. 8. Boston & New York: Houghton Mifflin, 1903–4).

Girshman, Roman, Vladimir Minorsky, and Ramesh Sanghvi. Photos by William McQuitty. *Persia: The Immortal Kingdom.* Greenwich, Conn.: New York Graphic Society, 1971.

Goethe, Johann Wolfgang. *West-Östlicher Divan: West-Eastern Divan.* von J. Whaley, translator. Munich: Deutscher Taschenbuch Verlag, 1979.

Golestan, Shahrokah. *The Wine of Nishapur: A Photographer's Promenade in the "Rubaiyat of Omar Khayyam."* English rendering by Karim Emami. Paris: Souffles, 1988.

Gray, Elizabeth T., Jr., trans. *The Green Sea of Heaven: Fifty Ghazals from the Diwan of Hafiz.* Ashland, Ore.: White Cloud Press, 1995.

Gray, John. *Near Eastern Mythology.* New York: Hamlyn, 1955.

Huxley, Aldous. *The Perennial Philosophy.* New York: Harper and Row, 1944.

Khan, Inayat and Coleman Barks. *The Hand of Poetry: Five Mystic Poets of Persia.* New Lebanon, N.Y.: Omega, 1993.

Levy, Reuben. *An Introduction to Persian Literature.* New York, London: Columbia University Press, 1969.

Mehr, Farhang. *The Zoroastrian Tradition: An Introduction to the Ancient Wisdom of Zarathustra.* Rockport, Mass.: Element, 1991.

Mendelsohn, Isaac, ed. *Religions of the Ancient Near East.* New York: Liberal Arts Press, 1955.

Middleton, Christopher, ed. *Goethe: The Collected Works,* Vol. 1. Princeton, N.J: Princeton University Press, 1983.

Montgomery, Roger. *Twenty Count.* Santa Fe, N. Mex.: Bear and Company, 1995.

Moulton, James Hope. *Early Zoroastrianism.* London: Williams & Norgate, 1913.

Payne, John. *The Poems of Shemseddin Mohammad Hafiz of Shiraz,* 3 vols. London: Privately published for the Villon Society, 1901.

Rasuli, Mohammad Mehdi. *Anarestan.* Paintings by Rasuli with Rumi translations by Behrouz Tourani. Tehran: Nashr-e-Sham Publishing, 1992.

Sarkhosh Curtis, Vesta. *Persian Myths: The Legendary Past.* Austin: University of Texas, 1993.

Shaw, Bernard. *Man and Superman: A Comedy and A Philosophy.* London: Penguin Books, 1957.

Shiva, Shahram T. *Rending the Veil: Literal and Poetic Translations of Rumi.* Prescott, Ariz.: Hohm Press, 1995.

Smith, Paul. *Book of the Winebringer: Masnavi of Hafiz.* Melbourne: New Humanity Books, 1986.

———. *Hafiz Tongue of the Hidden: Poems from the Divan.* Melbourne: New Humanity Books, 1986.

———. *Love's Perfect Gift: Rubaiyat of Hafiz.* Melbourne: New Humanity Books, 1986.

Streit, Claude K. *Hafiz, Tongue of the Hidden.* New York: Viking, 1928.

Tagore, Rabindranath. *The Religion of Man.* Boston: Beacon, 1931.

Time-Life Books. *Sumer: Cities of Eden.* Lost Civilizations Series. Alexandria, Va.: Time-Life Books, 1930.

Walters, I. Donald, editor. *The Rubaiyat of Omar Khayyam Explained by Paramahansa Yogananda.* Nevada City, Calif.: Crystal Clarity, 1994.

Whitemore, Hugh. *The Best of Friends.* Oxford: Amber Lane Press, 1988.

Willis, Roy, ed. *World Mythology.* New York: Henry Holt, 1993.

Yogananda, Paramahansa. *Wine of the Mystic: The Rubaiyat of Omar Khayyam, A Spiritual Interpretation.* Los Angeles: Self-Realization Fellowship, 1995.

Farsi Bibliography

Afshar, Iraj, ed. *Divan-e Kohne-ye Hafez* (The Old Divan of Hafez). Tehran: Amir Kabir Publishing, 1969.

Akbari Hamed, Mehdi. *Hafézaneha-ye Arabi* (Hafez's Arabic Verses). Tehran: Self-published, 1987.

Bamdad, Mohammad Ali. *Hafez Shenasi* (Mastering Hafez). Tehran: Ebn-e Sina Publishing, 1960.

Dashti, Ali. *Kakh-e Ebdaa* (The Palace of Creativity). Tehran: Bonyad-e Farhang-e Iran Publishing, 1978.

———. *Naghshi az Hafez* (An Image of Hafez). Tehran: Asatir Publishing, 1965.

Ghani, Ghassem. *Bahs dar Asar va Afkar va Ahval-e Hafez* (A Discussion on the Works, Thoughts, and Feelings of Hafez. Vol. 1: The History of Hafez's Times; Vol. 2: The History of Sufism in Islam), Tehran: Zavvar Publishing, 1941).

Ghazvini, Allameh and Ghassem Ghani. *Divan-e Hafez* (The Divan of Hafez). Tehran: Arvin Publishing, 1994.

Heravi, Hossein-Ali. *Sharh-e Ghazalha-ye Hafez* (An Explanation of Hafez's Ghazals), 4 vols. Tehran: Nashr-e No Publishing, 1988.

Hooman, Mahmood. *Hafez*. Tehran: Tahouri Publishing, 1978.

Islami Nadushan, Mohammad Ali. *Majaraye Payan Napazir-e Hafez* (The Endless Adventure of Hafez). Tehran: Yazdan Press, 1995.

Izadi, Reza, ed. *Divan-e Khajeh Shams-ud-Din Mohammad Hafez-e Shirazi* (Divan of Hafez). Tehran: Eshraghi Publishing, 1993.

Jalali Naïni, Mohammad Reza and Nazir Ahmad, editors. *Divan-e Khajeh Shams-ud-din Mohammad Hafez-e Shirazi* (The Divan of Hafez of Shiraz). Tehran: Amir Kabir Publishing, 1973.

Khatib Rahbar, Khalil, ed. *Divan-e Ghazaliat-e Molana Shams-ud-Din Mohammad Khajeh Hafez-e Shirazi* (Divan of Molana Hafez of Shiraz). Tehran: Safi Ali Shah Publishing, 1995.

Khorramshahi, Baha-ud-Din. *Zehn o Zaban-e Hafez* (The Mind and Language of Hafez), 5th ed. Tehran: Moïn Publishing, 1995.

———. *Hafez,* 2nd ed. Tehran: Tarhé No Publishing, 1995.

———. *Hafeznameh* (Letters of Hafez), 2 vols. Tehran: Elmi va Farhangi Publishing, 1987.

——— and Mohammad Niknam. *Bargozideh va Sharh-e Hafez* (Hafez: Selected Poems and Explanations). Tehran: Farzan Publishing, 1994.

Mahmoudi Bakhtiari, Ali-Gholi. *Rahi be Maktab-e Hafez* (A Path to the School of Hafez). Tehran: Self-published, 1966.

Mallah, Hossein-Ali. *Hafez va Musighi* (Hafez and Music). Tehran: Honar va Farhang Publishing, 1972.

Mazareï, Fakhr-ud-Din. *Mafhoum-e Rendi dar Shéer-e Hafez* (The Meaning of Rendi in Hafez's Poetry). Tehran: Kavir Publishing, 1994.

Moïn, Mohammad. *Hafez-e Shirin Sokhan* (The Sweet-Tongued Hafez), Vols. 1 and 2, Tehran: Moïn Publishing, 1990.

Mortazavi, Manouchehr. *Maktab-e Hafez* (The School of Hafez), 2nd ed. Tehran: Tous Publishing, 1987.

Natel Khanlari, Parviz, ed. *Divan-e Hafez Khajeh Shams-ud-Din Mohammad* (Divan of Khajeh Hafez), 2 vols. Tehran: Kharazmi Publishing, 1983.

Neysari, Salim, ed. *Divan-e Ghazalha-ye Hafez* (The Divan of Hafez's Ghazals). Tehran: Alhoda International, 1992.

Niknam, Mehrdad. *Ketabshenasi-ye Hafez* (A Bibliography of Hafez). Tehran: Elmi va Farhangi Publishing, 1988.

Parizi, Bastani. *Shah Mansur* (King Mansur). Tehran: Khorram Publishing, 1991.

Partow Alavi, Abdol-Ali. *Bang-e Jaras* (Call of the Bell). Tehran: Kharazmi Publishing, 1970.

Pejman, Hossein, editor. *Divan-e Molana Shams-ud-Din Mohammad Hafez* (Divan of Hafez). Tehran: Borukhim Publishing, 1936.

Rahimi, Mostafa. *Hafez-e Andisheh* (The Hafez of Thought). Tehran: Nour Publishing, 1992.

Rouh-ul-Amini, Mahmoud. *Bavarha-ye Amianeh Dar Bare-ye Fal-e Hafez* (Common Beliefs About Hafez's Oracle). Tehran: Pajang Publishing, 1990.

Saremi, Esmail, editor. *Yaddashtha-ye Doctor Ghassem Ghani dar Havashi-ye Divan-e Hafez* (Dr. Ghassem Ghani's Notes on the Margins of Hafez's Divan). Tehran: Elmi Publishing, 1987.

Sayeh, editor. *Hafez*. Tehran: Karnameh Publishing, 1995.

Sarvar Molaï, Mohammad. *Tajalli-e Ostoureh dar Divan-e Hafez* (The Luster of Mythology in Hafez's Divan). Tehran: Tous Publishing, 1989.

Zaryab Khoï, Abbas. *Ayineh-e Jam* (Mirror of the Grail). Tehran: Elmi Publishing, 1989.

Zarrinkoub, Abdol-Hossein *Az Kouche-ye Rendan* (From the Passageway of the Rends). Tehran: Sokhan Publishing, 1995.

Zonnour, Rahim. *Dar Jastojou-ye Hafez* (In Search of Hafez), 2 vols. Tehran: Zavvar Publishing, 1983.

Index

The Writing Team

As a child in her native Iran, Haleh Pourafzal (1956–2002) came to know the poetry and spirit of Haféz through her father and her extended family. One of her favorite prayer sites was the poet's beautiful tomb in his home city, Shiraz. Haleh came to America at age seventeen and earned a Master's Degree in International Development from Clark University. She served as a director for several years with Oxfam America, the international relief and development agency. Her work included hands-on community empowerment in Africa, Asia, Latin America, and the Middle East. Her poetry, translations, and other writings have been published internationally. During her final month before crossing into the Realm of Spirit, Haleh completed work on a new videotape about Haféz. The tape is being shown both at the site of the poet's tomb in Shiraz, where she once prayed, and also to schoolchildren throughout Iran to acquaint them with their rich cultural heritage.

Abdol-Hossein Pourafzal, Haleh's father, served as the literary consultant for this book. A guest lecturer on Persian language, literature and poetry at the Sorbonne University in Paris, he is a fifth generation direct descendent of Ghaem Magham Farahani, creator of the contemporary Farsi prose form. The Pourafzal family lineage traces back 1,500 years and includes many mystics, artists, and educators.

Coauthor Roger Montgomery, Haleh's husband, is also the author of *Twenty Count*, the story of a search for self-knowledge as guided by an ancient Mesoamerican spiritual system. During their thirteen years together, Haleh and Roger worked as consultants with individuals and groups committed to creating environments that nurture justice, service, and sustainability. Their work served international and domestic clients whose missions range from poverty and homelessness to consciousness research.

Books of Related Interest

Rumi: Gazing at the Beloved
The Radical Practice of Beholding the Divine
by Will Johnson

Journey to the Lord of Power
A Sufi Manual on Retreat
by Ibn 'Arabi

The Way of Sufi Chivalry
by Ibn al-Hasayn al-Sulami

The Book of Sufi Healing
by Shaykh Hakim Moinuddin Chishti

Islamic Patterns
An Analytical and Cosmological Approach
by Keith Critchlow

Shambhala
In Search of the New Era
by Nicholas Roerich

The Arabic Parts in Astrology
A Lost Key to Prediction
by Robert Zoller

Inner Traditions • Bear & Company
P.O. Box 388
Rochester, VT 05767
1-800-246-8648
www.InnerTraditions.com

Or contact your local bookseller